It's Not a Chore. It's Evolution

It's Not a Chore. It's Evolution, Volume 1

Michelle Syner

Published by Claw and Clover Books, 2024.

While every precaution has been taken in the preparation of this book, the publisher assumes no responsibility for errors or omissions, or for damages resulting from the use of the information contained herein.

IT'S NOT A CHORE. IT'S EVOLUTION

First edition. March 31, 2024.

ISBN: 979-8224664092

Written by Michelle Syner.

Table of Contents

SELF LOVE AND JUDGEMENT 1

ASCENTION & EVOLUTION 13

BEING YOUR AUTHENTIC SELF 28

MANIFESTING AND THE FUTURE 43

AWARENESS AND THE MATRIX 59

GROUNDING AND BEING PRESENT 74

CONTROL AND THE FLOW 85

WORKING WITH OTHERS 99

INCORPORATING THE PAST 117

SHADOW WORK.. 126

ACTIONS EQUAL RESULTS... 143

RUTS AND STAYING MOTIVATED 154

LEARNING AND SHIFTING.. 170

POETRY 185

This book is dedicated to Alice Alicja Jones, my mentor and friend. She has helped push me through my blockages, recognize when my Guides were speaking to me, and provided me with the tools and encouragement to continue to connect, which lead to the messages in this book. Without her guidance and perspective, this book would not exist.

Prologue

You only know what you know when you know it. Part of personal development and spiritual work is coming into that awareness and putting in the time and effort to try to understand the world around you seen and unseen. I had gotten to that point in my adult life where I was aware guides existed and that we could connect with them. The question then became how. And with any question the internet had an answer. I took courses, listened to lectures, guided meditations, even a writing assignment from my Spiritual mentor that involved writing every day for 180 days and going back and looking for where the tone changed. I was getting frustrated as it didn't seem to be working.

I kept coming back to when I was a teenager and would write poetry and kept a journal. I remember the words would just flow sometimes. I referred to it as stream of consciousness writing, where I'd just let go and free associate words and they'd just keep coming. The pages would basically write themselves. So, I started a new notebook to try to get the words to flow again like they used to. I let it become more organic.

I had a session with my mentor and asked if my guides had any messages for me. She said they were frustrated that I wasn't listening to them. I conveyed that, it's kind of hard to if I don't know how to hear them. She tried to give me that same writing assignment again and I explained that I was keeping a journal. She again explained to go back through the entries to see where the tone changed. I then had a realization that one of my recent entries didn't seem like my writing. I went back through, and sure enough, I found where the tone changed. When I was writing it came from the first person. When my guides were coming through the tone went to second and third person.

Once I was able to recognize when they were coming through, it took me less than a week to learn how to connect directly, hold that connection, and even be able to ask questions during the transmission. I've been channel writing daily with them for a couple of years and have decided the messages serve no purpose if they aren't shared. This is the first book. There are more books to come as I continue to connect. The messages change as my journey evolves.

The name of the book comes from one of the entries. It's not a chore, it's evolution. There's a lot that goes into changing old defaults and habits once you bring into the light what needs to be addressed. It often seems like work, but it's really part of your personal evolution. This book is very personal to me as it's my actual journey in life and the advice my Spirit Guides are giving me along the way to keep me focused, motivated, and provide some much-needed insight when I'm feeling overwhelmed or lost.

Below is the journal entry that tipped me off during that call with my mentor and started this whole journey. It only seems fitting for this to be included in the introduction. As you go through this book remember take what resonates with you and leave what doesn't. Everyone's journey is different, it's about asking yourself the questions and seeing where you land.

Do you see? Can you see the truth? Do you know who you are yet? Can you find the path and tread it like It's your own, like you've been here before so many times but a few miles further... closer, ever closer to the truth, to the light, to the clearing, to the place you can finally call home.

You aren't mobile. You are freedom for being able to travel and to do what it is you need to do, not tied down or guilty about pursuing your path. Can't you see how this was set up for you? Once you stepped out and back into yourself, we had to cover ground, bring back what you lost, or temporarily forgot. But it's still there, you are just rusty. But you'll shine bright, make it new, improved by what you have gained. Then you can share and help guide. You are relatable due to your journey. You get it which makes you approachable and down to earth, though you are of the stars. You will shine so bright once you stop hiding in the shadows.

You must learn your expansion but also the limitations of your journey. You aren't meant to help them all. Some are not here for that this time. They have other lessons, other paths they are to travel. Let them go their way, they are not your hurdle. You keep growing and stay the course. You are too sensitive yet. You need to let go. Don't judge yourself based on others. They are not ready. You are. Shine so others can see. Be that light for those that need it.

You have compassion and love. You never closed your heart despite the hurt. You held out faith on the betterment of who they could be, or actually are if not for the Ego and their work. You can only be a shoulder. They still need to do the work. That is not on you, and it is not your burden. Take with you what you learned and apply it in your own special way. Teach and lead and they will follow you. They can see your heart, the broach on your sleeve. Shine like your jewelry. Be even brighter. Just be you. You've got this.

SELF LOVE AND JUDGEMENT

Worthiness... Are you paying attention to what you are listening to? That's another one of those items you need to work on. You struggle with your value and your worth. You've gotten better but there is still a part of you that shrinks aways or feels not as important as others. As you start to speak your truth, you will be able to address this. When you have confidence in what you have to say and stop worrying about how others will react or if what you say or do is offending them, you are finding your worth.

You are worthy of having your own ideas and options. You are worthy of being respected enough for others to listen and hear you out. You don't need to adapt what you have to say to please others. You need to be truthful not watered down. That's part of living your authentic self. Find your truth. Speak it. Share it. Don't be ashamed of it. You don't need to hide who you are from others and only be yourself in the quiet confines of your home. You already know who you are. You need to connect and share that with others. It gives them permission to be themselves, and opens the door for real, honest connections on a much deeper level. It allows everyone to let go of fear, respect each other, and speak their truth.

Don't get too comfortable in mediocrity. You weren't meant to disappear in the background. You aren't meant to observe life, but participate in it, and actually make it happen. Live your life. Don't just sit back and watch it go by, then look back with regret. If you lived in your present, you would build a more enjoyable future. Don't let it pass you by. Take advantage of everything you are given, every opportunity, every interaction. You can't have those if you stay at home and confine yourself within these walls.

You create your own prison and get comfortable there but forget that you have the keys. You are free and can leave at any time. Where should you go? It doesn't really matter. Just get out there. When you leave, your mind thinks differently. You live differently. Your vibration changes. Life could be an adventure.

We don't understand how you all read books and watch movies about other people's adventures and life experiences and get upset when it ends. You are living vicariously through characters. You could just live those lives yourself instead of reading about them. You just need to take the initiative and go out there and do something. When you look back at your most memorable moments are you remembering being at home watching tv or are you remembering being out in the world experiencing life, interacting with people, creating new memories? You need to remember an action or inaction is what's creating the life you live. Do you want to create memories or stay at home?

Yes, rest when you need to. Regroup and have your time for reflection. But when you do that as your sole activity, you are losing something. You need to find balance between activities and reflection. Between connecting in this plane and connecting with yourself on our plane. Your feet need to be in both locations to have balance, to feel that harmony, and get the most out of this experience.

You have to live a spiritual and physical life. It's not one or the other. One enhances the other. We are all learning lessons through your time on this plane. If you aren't going out there and interacting, we are losing something along with you. Get out there, remember the promises you made to yourself of being more social or having a car so you can go on adventures. Your adventures start now. Get out there.

———————————

IT'S NOT A CHORE. IT'S EVOLUTION

Sponsor yourself. Invest in yourself. You are worth it. You need to support your own dreams and journey. If you don't believe in yourself, no one else will. Change will happen. It will feel like a surprise to some, but others who have gotten to know you or can sense your spirit will understand and be excited for you. Hold onto those that are excited about your progress. They will be the support you need when you get down on yourself. Things won't always run smoothly, that's just how learning and implementing something new goes. You are re-training your default settings to do something new and that takes time. But you must make those changes to fully incorporate them into the life you are building.

You get to be an architect. You'll have help but ultimately you are designing this. We are the clients helping to push the limits of what's possible and making your dream bigger. You just need to make it happen, using your resources and skills and designing it in a way that only you can. But this future you are building still takes time, but you need to keep taking action to get there.

You are still struggling with self-esteem. You see where others are and their resources and start to compare and get concerned about yours. Sometimes there is value in understanding how they got to their destination in case there is something you haven't thought of. But their journey is not yours. You have different resources and motivations, different connections, and support groups. There are a lot of different factors that go into the success of each person even if one of the goals is the same for both of you, because the journey is not. The lessons are not. Don't concern yourself with how "others" might have it easier. Their milestones might stop long before the ones you need to reach. You are going further; your path continues past where they stop, and you have completion.

You also don't understand how much effort they put in. You might have more available time than they do, but they use their time to the fullest. You seem to burn out quicker. Again, not trying to put you down but you need to find the source of why you are exhausted all the time. Why do you lose your motivation. Why do you feel depressed or not good enough. Until you start to address these things, they will continue to block your progress.

You need to come from a place of self-love. You keep forgetting. You get caught up in going through the motions and to do lists that you are leaving yourself out of the equation and the "things" are taking center stage. You start to not enjoy your life. You forget who you are and why you are here. You forget how to make yourself happy when you are not able to make time for you. What are you going through all of this for? Find your answers. Find your purpose. How do you want to feel through your day?

You get so caught up on what you still need to accomplish or what's going wrong. Then you are judging yourself instead of coming from a place of love. Your interactions become necessities and inconveniences instead of loving connections. Stop and see what you are doing and where you are coming from. If you can't love yourself then everything you do will come from the wrong perspective. You are capable of so much when you come back to your heart center. When you are happy your spark returns, and people see that. What are you missing? What makes you happy? What time can you devote to your self-care? Make sure your self-care isn't something that brings you down or you judge yourself for. Self-care is not judgement, it's self-love and everyone needs to be shown love.

IT'S NOT A CHORE. IT'S EVOLUTION

Desires to be heard or seen, what do you have to say? What is its importance? Is it important to you or the recipient of the conversation? Know yourself before you know your audience. Where is this coming from within and what is the end goal? What are you trying to discover, share, or celebrate? You need to believe it first or it falls dead on the audience. You can't turn it on and off like a light and talk about incorporating it into your daily life. Is it part of your life? Part of who you are? If so, why does it feel ignored? Look within and see where you fall short, what you could be doing to make the narrative correct. You must buy it yourself before you can sell it to others.

Be honest with yourself. Visualizing what you want to see that is not present now, is not lying to yourself about your reality. It's an openness and willingness to let go of this reality for a better one that serves you. You can still accept this reality while visualizing the new one. You just need to work on not lingering and holding on to your frustrations that hold you to this one when visualizing how you'd rather do things. Be honest with yourself in that you don't believe you could have more, and that **this** is what is holding you back. Be honest with what you still need to work on or let go of to move forward. Be honest in where you are holding yourself back so that you can address it. Then handle it and start to make your move. You need to be the one to dig yourself out of the hole you fell into, one shovelful at a time. Do the work. Make progress. Free yourself.

You must see your worth for progress to happen. Do you believe in yourself enough to visually see good in your life or is that still difficult for you? Do you believe and know you deserve better and that lack and struggle are not who you are as a person. It's just something that was passed down to you, and it's time to let it go. Let your family continue to believe that's how they should live but you choose the life you want and how you want to show up for yourself. Those days of struggle are your past. Leave them there. We are building new and setting new habits and self-talk in place. You can be prosperous. You just need to believe it for yourself to own it in your life. If you are still viewing it as "oh that would be nice", instead of "yes that's me" then you aren't there yet. You are still viewing it as unattainable instead of already received. It makes a difference. One is a dream; one is a new reality. Do you want to dream or to become?

Take care of yourself and then show up for yourself. You need to be determined and not back burner your life and what you want to see in your life. Are you worth your own time and investment or not? Find out why you are still not believing what you want to see. Break through those restraints and set yourself free. You have a life to live and it's waiting for you.

———————

Break through, come free. There is still something holding you back: hesitation, disbelief in results. You emotionally don't believe and aren't surprised when you get negative results. Flip them. Dig in and dig deep. Then focus on the shift. Meditation is more than clearing your mind for a couple of minutes. Work past the clearing into the connecting part. You pull out too quickly and get distracted too often to make it there. That's where you can find answers. That's where peace lies. But you need to practice, persist, and push through your not feeling worthy enough to get there.

Loving yourself is the key to a lot of the struggles you have. If you loved yourself, you would feel worthy of that which you seek. But there is a part of you still saying you aren't meant to have abundance; you aren't meant to be seen. You need to let go of that belief. It's not yours and it's not helpful. Staying small does you no favors, or any of those whose lives you affect. Stretch out, take up space. You know the difference between being cocky and being confident so don't assume the worst. You've learned lessons. You have understanding. You are limiting yourself and not in a good way. Remove the chains and break free. You have more to offer and need to put yourself out there. Be free and invite the changes that come. You have more to be than this.

———

Be social. Break up the routine. See what conversations can enhance your perspective or how your spark can light other's way. You are a catalyst anytime you interact with others. You don't need to be alone for progress to occur. Sometimes the opportunities are outside of your comfort zone and stepping out is the only way you'll have that access. Be aware of your thoughts and what you try to talk yourself out of and why. Are you stunting your own growth? Are you getting in your own way? What if you just lived in the moment instead of judging it or looking for something more? What if you were just present and that was enough?

Not everything is a step. Some things are seeds being planted for later development. Just relax and let be. It's not a scavenger hunt that needs to be sorted out. Be in the moment and let it unfold the way it's supposed to. Just observe or experience and be present. You are allowed to just enjoy life sometimes too. View each day as a new opportunity. Start it in an optimistic mood and let it be positive. Don't drag it down due to sleep, circumstances, or the weather. Those are the details. Let the overall picture develop. It's ok if some of the pieces are damaged. You still need them to see the whole. Just keep going and be open to how things unfold without judgement but with curiosity. You'll enjoy your day more this way.

———

Pace yourself. If you feel stressed that's on you for taking on too much or rushing yourself. You set your own schedule and your own pace. If it doesn't work, pause, and see why. Are you in the moment or worrying about what needs to be done next? There is no stress in the present. Stress is from overthinking and jumping to other things. Slow yourself down and enjoy what you are doing and the choices you made for the day. The things you do should bring you joy. If they don't, check your perspective and what's really happening.

Be open to new thoughts and perspectives. There's a difference between knowing what your objective is and what works for you and accepting help and better ideas. It does not mean you are a failure in your attempts but are open to better solutions. Everything can be approved upon, and sometimes you don't have all the answers. What do you need to work on and how do you want to do that work? Don't get lost in the how. Try a few different methods or ideas and see what resonates. Don't just get frustrated and give up or move to other things. It may not come easily right now, but once you realize what works and what's holding you back it'll make everything easier.

Stop comparing yourself to others. They are where they are for different reasons and have had different journeys. Also, they had more years and different finances for the same things. You can't compare a 60-year-old to a 40-year-old. A lot is different in those 20 years. It's like comparing a baby to a college student. It's different times. Just be where you are. Do what you can with what you have and be patient or work for the rest. It's not your time yet, but that doesn't mean it's not coming.

Rest when you need to. Part of self-awareness is also listening to your body and what it needs and taking care of your health. It's not about forcing yourself to do things to an unhealthy level. It's about balance and harmony. Make progress yes, but not at the expense of your health.

IT'S NOT A CHORE. IT'S EVOLUTION

You can't make progress if you are sick or bedridden. You need to be loving and gentle to yourself too, not just to others. Care about yourself and your health. Take time off for recovery if you need instead of pushing yourself too hard and wondering why you feel run down. How are you treating yourself? Are you treating yourself like a failure when your body needs down time, or are you understanding and appreciate that you recognize you need rest, and it has benefits too?

Love is not just for others. You are included in the whole and need shown compassion even by yourself. How you treat yourself reflects how you are able to treat others. Is your kindness just on the surface or is it a part of your character? Where are your motives? How do you really feel? What are you gaining from showing compassion? Be honest with yourself and see where you stand on loving yourself. You need to love yourself in the down days as well as the good days. You can't pick and choose. You need unconditional love too and what better place to get it than from yourself? Start there and see how it changes everything around you.

———

Everyday can be a fresh start to implement change and update your life. What do you want to be aware of? What would you like to change? How would you like to try harder? You don't need a special day to do better but if you have one to use as a starting point it could help you with keeping track. You are starting a new year on this plane. How did this last year go? What worked and what didn't? Where can improvements be made?

Love doesn't have to be a word. It's actions and expression. It can be shown in how you treat people, where you place priorities, how you handle them with care. Someone can show you without saying it. Yet someone can say it and not show it or mean it. It's not a word. It's more tangible than an expression of compassion and respect. Who is showing it to you? Who is saying it but doesn't mean it? It's not so fleeting when it's real. Do you love someone else more than you love yourself? Are you able to show yourself the same compassion you show others? Are you lying to yourself or being honest? Are you being supportive and understanding or judging and getting angry? You need to show up for yourself the same as you would for someone else you love. You should play favorites and you should be on the top of that list.

You don't need a word if it has no meaning if it's just a thought and not an action. How sincere are the people you surround yourself with? Where do you fall in their priorities and where have you placed them in yours? Don't take it to heart. Just make note and adjust accordingly. This is how you prevent drama and hurt feelings. Be aware and notice the details and it'll start to make sense.

How much of your current life do you accept without judgement? It's one thing to know you want to work on or change an aspect of your life, but it's another to keep judging and not loving yourself because of where you are in comparison to where you want to be and your ability and determination to get there. Are you a supportive cheerleader to yourself or an angry parent making yourself feel like nothing you do is correct or good enough? Is how you talk to yourself come from love or hate? Is it a reflection of how you feel or are you taking over how others used to make you feel little or lacking? Notice how you encourage or discourage yourself. How does it affect your self-worth? How does it affect your results? Do you always feel not enough and lacking, or do you love yourself enough to accept where you are now and encourage growth but at whatever pace it shows up without judgment?

Do you accept yourself differently on good days vs what you consider a bad day? Where is your love going? Is it only for others or do you show love and compassion to yourself as well? Do you feel worthy of love?

IT'S NOT A CHORE. IT'S EVOLUTION

Do you feel like a qualifier is necessary to receive love? If you do this or achieve that then I will validate and show you love and respect. Do you treat yourself the same or worse than you treat those you care about? If it's worse, why is that? If you can't support or accept yourself then how can you expect others to? Lead by example. Treat yourself correctly and expect others to come up to that same level in how they interact with you. How much acceptance and grace are you going to give to yourself today?

How much do you trust yourself and your decisions? Do you trust your own judgement, or do you constantly need validation? It's one thing to go within or ask your guides. But it's another to never trust yourself and need an outside party to confirm or validate decisions you need to make for the direction of your life. You need to start to trust that you know where you are going and how to get there. Even the scary choices are ones you can trust yourself to make. There are times that you will need to ask someone with more experience or knowledge on a topic for advice but in your normal day-to-day processes, how independent are you?

You need to make sure that you aren't still in default mode from being in controlling relationships in your past. You've been in positions where you were made to feel every step you took was wrong and needed permission. That can cause hesitation on self-belief. Make sure you have released that. Make sure you know you are capable. Confirm for yourself that you know what's best for you despite what other's views might be on how they'd do something. This is your life. Live it how you want to. You know what you need to work on, where you don't want to be, and what is a step backwards or a leap forward. Trust in yourself and your inner knowledge. You are stronger and more capable than you give yourself credit for. Remind yourself how far you have come without the help of others, figuring it out as you go. Pull on that strength again whenever you need it. You have a truth inside that is perfect for you. Find it and trust it.

Find ways to make life work for you. It is here to teach you, support you, and let you express yourself. But you must decide how you view it or use the resources you were given. Are you determined enough to lead or guide your life in the direction you want, or are you comfortable and complacent? You can daydream all you want. But that's all they are, dreams, if efforts and actions don't follow those thoughts. You could live those dreams if you really tried, if you really believed, if it were your goal.

How worthy of your own dreams do you think you are? Are you talking yourself out of change due to not feeling "enough"? Where is that coming from? You are capable of so much and are stronger than you realize. Don't sell yourself short before you even begin. You are a creator. You can manifest the life you desire. Is your belief in yourself holding you back? Are your resources holding you back? Are you addressing any of your roadblocks or are you just stopping and turning the car around and going back from which you came?

Don't spend your life in fear or regret. Don't live a life that is mediocre and does not drive you or make you feel alive. You are worthy of the life you dream of. It will take effort and some time, but it is better than the alternative which is just going through the same routine every day until death. Is this really living? Is this what your experience amounts to for you? Care about yourself enough to seek new paths. Explore, inquire, make the changes needed to pursue your personal happiness. You'll be glad you did.

ASCENTION & EVOLUTION

How bad do you want it? How much work are you willing to put in? Is it considered work if it's what you want, what you are meant to do? It's not a chore. It's evolution. It's adapting to change. You are growing, sprouting, becoming who you are. Who you were. Who you were meant to be.

Being, It's part of you. It's inside of you. It is you. Maybe you just haven't sorted it out yet. Though it's what you came here for. It's for the betterment of man. It's for the betterment of yourself. Resistance is a hurtle, Jump over it. Keep going. Make it to the finish line. Don't give up or give in. Go within or be without. It's up to you. Will you take advantage of the situation you are given, or give up on the chance to be grand, to be bigger than where you are, to live life to its fullest?

Full of wonder, joy, and love. Love yourself, then love others. You'll get there, but you need to put in the effort, the time. It's not much we ask, but you need to take the steps to get to your destination.

We aren't trying to inconvenience you, but you need to catch up. We are losing time and want you to succeed at what you came here to do. It's too big for you to grasp at the present which is why we are implementing steps and adding more when you are ready. The big picture would scare you at this point because you are not at a level of seeing your own potential, and your ego is trying to shut you down from something it doesn't have control over.

You need to take back control. This life is yours to live, not yours to scrape by and be mediocre in. That is not why you were incarnated. You did not come here to fall in line, to be a robot in the machine of the

3rd dimensional illusion of littleness and preconceived notions of what others feel "living" is.

You came here to be a catalyst for change, to lay the brickwork for the evolution of the planet, to keep expanding the possibilities of all. I know you are thinking, how can one person expand a planet, but you aren't one person. You are backed by an army that knows what you are capable of and knows how you can trigger others, tapping into their internal army. You can all then march together into a new future, a new dimension, a new shift for the planet, for the species, for mankind.

You are a catalyst for change. It's not changing you. It's remembering who you are and tapping into that to remind others of their limitlessness. We must start. We must keep going. There will be others who join you. You are not alone in this mission. They will enter the story when it is time and you will know when you meet them, as they will seem familiar, like a different version of you.

You know what that connection feels like, you have had it before. You are familiar and you will succeed in connecting those dots that need connected to smooth the lines and build the picture of what can be.

You aren't starting late. You are starting at the time when you were ready. You needed to learn what you learned for this to make sense and to remove the distractions that would prevent you from allowing yourself to be more than you thought you were capable of. You got this and will understand it better in time. It will all make sense as you go, as you learn, as those parts are getting activated, and the change happens. The change is coming. You just need to keep moving along with it.

————————

What are you going to do to make a difference on this planet? Change needs to happen on a global scale. People are becoming activated due to the problems and injustices. When things are run by the few or with the wrong priorities it's time for a change. Entire countries can't continue to be stuck when they are the majority, and the problem is just a few people. Stop giving control to those who would abuse it.

Yes, education plays a part. When blinders are on, or you are distracted by something else that you don't understand, that makes for the perfect recipe for being able to be controlled. You must be vigilant in your thought process and who benefits from situations. There are a lot of self-serving people in positions that are to be serving the public which does not work.

The pandemic is almost over. It's winding down. There's only a little longer to go. Things will not go back to normal. Changes were needed to help bring light and force the hand. There was also a density of the plane that needed adjusted. Don't feel bad for those who left from this. They had agreed before incarnation. Some to help others. Some for realizations on this journey.

Adjust your antenna, connect when you need to. There is not a set time or set purpose, if you have questions or we have advice. It's just about connecting and making time. Where do you prioritize this? What value do you receive? This is for your personal growth. We don't need you to become dependent and stop making your own decisions. We are here to guide you, not run your life. We are here to advise not dictate the how.

You are at least on the right path, so you can't get frustrated with yourself. You have had several breakthroughs and have stepped out of your bubble to make changes. Give yourself credit where credit is due. We don't view time as you do. So, it's different from this end. Just keep going and ask the questions, seek the answers, implement changes, and see the results. Keep doing what you are doing. The next steps will come. Don't stress trying to figure it out or control things. We are trying to break you of your need to control. Life becomes easier when you let go and move with the flow instead of trying to march determined into the future. You could be marching the wrong way, allocating your troops and supplies to the wrong battles. Fighting instead of living. Take a step back, realize when you are doing this. Find a way to shift out of it, to improve, to let go, to let life unfold as it should. There would be less damage control if you would just stop viewing things as battles to be won and saw them as just parts of life, experiences to be had.

Release the worry. You have taken the next steps, wait and see how it unfolds. You can't do anything about it now so why think of negative scenarios? Have we not seen things turn out ok and then realize how much time you wasted in negative scenario building for nothing? Be in the moment, not dreading infinite possibilities of things that could go wrong. What if they could go right? What if that's the outcomes you should be focusing on? Why do you need to foreshadow an outcome anyway? Just let it be and adjust when results are received. There is peace in not knowing sometimes.

Everything feels like an opposite because you are trying to find balance in life. There is no right or wrong, or good or bad. It's a shifting of perspective and gaining knowledge from lessons and awareness. You can't keep getting frustrated. Transitions and breaking habits take time. Your awareness of the habits is what you are frustrated about because it puts to light what you still need to address. How you address it and how long it's going to take is not something you have much control over. How you address it yes, but how long, no.

IT'S NOT A CHORE. IT'S EVOLUTION

You need to be patient with yourself and others as this new awareness surfaces and the things that aren't serving you come up. It seems like a constant because a lot has come to surface at once and is still not been diffused. Don't overwhelm. Choose one at a time to place your focus and start to work on it. Make the work consistent. Shadow work can be completed the same way. Yes, you need to meditate and stay there, not get scared or bored when you start to connect. You are still holding yourself back. There's a part of you that is full steam ahead, but another part of you dragging its feet and refusing to come along on the journey. You need to ask yourself why. Set that part at ease. Hear it out. Find out why and get on board. You can't set sail with an anchor still down.

You could learn more, but you need to handle those blockages first or you'll be filtering the correspondence to stay within your boundaries of knowledge. If you don't know a subject, then understanding it or us proving correct name or words is an issue, because you need to write it down and won't hear it right if it's not a part of your vocabulary. You are still filtering this correspondence to a point. The message is ours, but the wording and adjustments are still part of you.

It's a different channel than if we were to take over and use your physical body to speak or scribe directly. You aren't there yet and if you want to go that route it will take time. Even what you do vs your friend is different and accesses different information. One is not better than the other. But spirit meets you where you are. She put in more effort for much longer time and goes inward and can find that spot quickly. You can connect to the frequencies and feel that aspect quickly and she can't without a different effort. It's different gifts for different paths. Obviously, you can learn and improve and start to be able to connect better, but it's not a competition.

You'll be drawn to where you need to put your focus and what aspects you need to incorporate. You need to remain open and remove the blockages. You are still adding speed bumps and feeling like you are doing damage when you hit things at full speed. Slow down and find new paths to avoid those blockages. You won't go far in a broken vehicle. Fix the direction if you can't fix the road.

The shift is the transition of the planet. Changes that are happening globally are meant to set things back on the correct course for evolution needed on all levels. This has been set into action but has been elevated with who has been sent to the planet and what life courses have been activated. Even nature and disease are a part of the process to remove obstructions to help prepare for the evolutionary shift that is needed.

There are things happening on multiple planes and levels. It's not a small task. It's not something that can be completed in a few years. It takes time but a larger number of changes are happening in your lifetime. You will see a different world from your childhood and your final years. It's almost an all-hands-on deck situation to get the work that is needed done.

Several people have been activated to push toward their calling and not just surviving on this physical plane. You will start to see an uprising of those on a spiritual path, on an environmental preservation path, and the peacekeepers. There will be a lot of issues brought to the surface, but that's the only way people will be aware of what is broken to start the processes needed to finally fix the systems that are not working.

It will feel like it's getting worse before it gets better due to finding all the things that need fixed. The process might seem slow but when you look at the last 100 years, you'll realize how quick progress is by comparison. Everyone has a role to play, a gift to share, a lesson that needs to be incorporated into the larger story. You must share your knowledge and help others along the way. Though there is a growing number of those coming into awareness of what is happening, there is still a lot of dense energies that are stuck in their way and blocking the flow that needs to happen.

It is not your responsibility to try to drag them into the light, but when they are ready to learn, be there to support that. You can't force someone's eyes open. They need to get there on their own, as frustrating as it might seem. Stubbornness is a crutch many use to try to maintain control of things that can't be controlled. Everyone has their own blockages and their own internal work.

You need to do your part. You need to remove your blockages and assist. Shine your light where it will best benefit all. You are a part of this story, this shift. You did not come to this planet at this time by accident. You have a role to play, and you've already started the journey. Stay focused and listen to within. You are a part of this for a reason and play a bigger role than you think. A candle can light an entire room, when given a chance to shine. Be the light. Be the fire. Make that change.

Time is moving faster than it used to. It's an illusion and as the veil is lifted that illusion shifts and feels different physically. Change is upon us, and it manifests in different ways. Things are speeding up and it can feel unsettling for those that are connected and can feel energy. You aren't imagining it. It is happening and will continue to happen. The shift has already begun. As you transition into a higher dimension where time doesn't exist, you are teetering between the two which makes it feel different and not as it was prior. Those further into the next dimension will feel it more than those grasping to the 3rd dimension.

There is also the illusion of when things are new, the experience will feel slower. Your childhood years, where it was constant learning, and you had no control, things seemed slow. But once you were working, formed routines, were looking forward to weekends and isolated events, you were wishing time to move faster as you were no longer living in the present as it was a chore. When you choose to view life as a chore and only find joy in future or isolated events, you are pushing your perspective of time to meet your needs. You look back and realize how much time has gone, and things have changed as you weren't present for them in the moment.

There are a few things happening with time and it's going to feel "off "as a result. But being aware of how you view time and how present you are at any given moment can help your perception of it. It allows you to ground yourself instead of feeling swept downstream by it. When you live for the future, you lose so much. Now is the only time you have. If you aren't using it wisely it will be gone, and you'll still be in the same place you were just older and unable to do as much as you wanted. We aren't saying push yourself to the point where you are overwhelmed but be aware of what you are doing and the choices you make.

If you look back and aren't happy, that's ultimately on you. This is your creation. You are the driver here. If you live your life pulled over on the side of the road, you aren't going to make it far. Life will keep going without you and you need to be present and contribute your part. You are a large part of the equation and need to be present to make the most of life.

Time does not need to feel scary. It's just a way to keep track of progress and milestones. It only has negative connotations when you label it as something other than a way to mark things down and keep track of them. Enjoy that you have it and that things take time so you can learn and make changes as you go. If everything was now, now, now, you would be overloaded because you are still learning what you want and how to get there. It's never too late to start again or set a new path. Every day could be a new start. It's all about how you want to view things and if you want to make the most of it or watch life pass you by.

It depends on your Contract and your goals as to what Ascended Masters are around you. Sometimes it's set up in spirit with how to best benefit you achieving your goals. They can also choose to help when awareness of where you are on your journey and what is needed comes to light. Your guides can pull them in. Or on your plane, if you become interested in a particular master, and call them into your life, they could enter then. They are always accessible at any stage needed. Never feel intimidated or like you are wasting their time when you want to connect but aren't sure what to ask for help on. On this level, they know what is needed and your restraints. Your higher self could be connecting on your behalf drawing you to them. There will be times you feel connected and aren't sure why.

The connections you have on all levels makes it hard to give a straight answer as there are so many options and circumstances. You could also select any master you feel drawn to once you learn about them from your plane. They aren't ego driven. They want to be known so that more have access to their assistance.

You have a lot of supporters on this side. Some are with you from the start. Some change up at different stages of your journey to help with different aspects. Some are loved ones that passed who are cheering you on, or your angels, your guides, friends, family, or Masters. If you ever feel alone, don't, because you are never truly alone. You just need to go within and connect on a different level. We are always accessible to you.

There is a bit of magic and intrigue involved in it. Getting excited about your awakening is a good sign. It helps keep you digging in and incorporating more into your life. Being curious and finding magic is the best place to be. We only worry with complacency, when you know there is more out there but shrug and go back to your physical life instead. You are not pulled into different aspects of your spiritual journey by mistake. You are drawn to what you need to learn, or refresh, or incorporate. You have synchronicities to help make sure you know something is important or to catch your attention and pull you back to the present. Pay attention to those signs and what we give you to catch your attention, even if it's just to pause and acknowledge. You could also write it down and ask questions when we connect if you aren't sure.

You are not on this journey alone. We are rooting for you and offering assistance. We are just as excited as you are to see you connecting and trying to clear the way for doing what you came here to do. Don't get discouraged or feel you are letting us down. You need to come from a place of non-judgement, even of yourself and what you are doing with your time. Yes, be aware and take accountability, but release the judgement and guilt and move on. Being frustrated with yourself and how you spend your time benefits no one. Get back on track when you are able and just keep going. You are still learning so it's understandable to still be fighting an uphill battle until you can find the flow and connect to it.

We want you to know we are with you, protecting and supporting you. We see your efforts and understand the struggles you are trying to resolve. We will support you however we can while you are working on making it through your self-doubt and paradigm shifts. There are times when you feel alone in this as it is an inward journey, but when you are focused on the journey you put other aspects of your life on hold to focus. Just remember to circle back and to incorporate a social life into the equation. Growth is sometimes unable to be seen until put into action during an interaction.

You are starting to realize how your social life slowly shifted to accommodate and meet you on your path. Your interactions are with your spiritual groups, those on a spiritual path, or those in service to others. Some of the others fall away or become acquaintances. You sometimes don't even notice the shift as it's gradual and has grown with you. Keep going where it leads. What do you really want is a hard question, when you know you don't want this, but you are still learning what is out there and don't know what opportunities are available. You can answer with a concept or a feeling. The goal will become clear as you learn more and find what feels correct. It does not mean you are directionless, just that you are keeping your options open.

Learn to speak up now that you are finding your voice. Exercise it. But do realize when it's ego or a paradigm speaking and not your heart. Why don't you want to do something? Is it that you really don't or that you are coming from a place of lack or a view of who you are not? Question things first then respond. Trusting your instinct is different than responding from your default settings. How does it make you feel? Learn the difference so you know which is speaking to you. Ask if you aren't sure but you will need to remove the safety net and learn to trust that feeling.

You are constantly shifting and changing the story of what your future could be. There is value in the work, the knowledge, and the time. Yes, sometimes you must sacrifice some aspects of your current life to have a new one. Pay attention to opportunities that are given to you. Don't be afraid to make changes if necessary. Obviously don't put yourself onto a sinking ship, make sure your vessel is secure before setting sail. But know when it's time to hit the seas, so you don't get caught in a storm and capsize. Use the judgment you are growing and obtaining and be patient and diligent. You are on the right path. Soak in the sun and keep going.

You are always connected. You just need to tune in. Never forget who you truly are. You don't need to pretend or to be something else. Just be you and you will shine and attract the right people. Those who don't understand are not on the same level and will fall away when it is time. Don't worry about them. This is how evolving happens. You must leave behind the old to step into the new. There cannot be change without releasing that which no longer serves you.

Holding on does not help you. It keeps you tethered to a place you are no longer in. Releasing does not mean giving up on something or that you can't maintain or don't love those you are leaving behind. It is you taking the steps forward that you need without the unnecessary restrictions and judgement that come from someone not on the same page, who is unable to realize that future and how it will benefit you. It does not make them bad people, just not as open and with more boundaries and limitations. They cannot see what they are not willing to open their eyes to. They have accepted where they are as permanent, and change would disrupt them. What they don't realize is change is the only constant and standing still won't stop that. Restricting other's growth won't change that. Only accepting the flow will allow you to live.

Going with the flow is simple yet hard because you need to be accountable for where you are holding yourself back and what boundaries you have imposed on yourself. You need to make those shifts. You need to do that work. You need to be accountable for yourself and the changes that need to happen. How you do that and how hard or easy the process is going to be is up to you. The first step is awareness, but once it is in the light you must acknowledge and do something about it. You can't be in the flow if you are concreted to the floor. You will just get battered and torn down as the flow will continue around you regardless. It will seem more difficult as a result, as the Universe is ready to incorporate you into the flow. You need to break free and move along with it.

Why are you scared? Why are you holding back? What do you need to step forward into your new life? These are your questions. Answer them honestly. If you can't be honest with yourself or find yourself making excuses or apologizing, that's an issue. Find the source. Clear the roots. Plant new seeds and bloom.

Looking for the positive does not mean wanting things back to before progress. Step out of your comfort zone. Your job is to find the balance of the new you are creating during the transition period, not look forward to the breaks when progress slows down. Shift how you view being busy by making better use of your time. Simplify the processes. Find your habits. What do you keep saying you'll work on but don't? You've already taken time away from one of your crutches, but did that gained time go to another? Be aware of what you are doing. You have your moments make them your new habits.

The messages will be at levels the person receiving understands. Guides are always with you. They are familiar with your mannerisms and how you process information. Someone with a scientific background is on a different level because that is what they are drawn to. So, their messages will be phrased more in line with how they talk. It doesn't mean their messages are more profound. They are just for a different audience. Your messages will be in a voice that would benefit you and will make sense to others on your level. Messages will also vary depending on what the guides are trying to help with and where the person's attention is. Many might be on spiritual paths, but just need different directions to get to their next stops, not destinations. You can still learn from each other's messages as it's all knowledge and remembering, which is universal, but the more specific steps for where you are headed will come from your instructors.

Learning is a form of remembering. This is why you get excited by certain content, or it resonates quicker. Sometimes you need to build for other information to make sense. You can't have a child learning to count do Calculus. They aren't there yet. So don't get discouraged when advanced levels don't click. You are just in a different class learning the groundwork still. It doesn't mean you won't get it someday. But if you are interested in something in particular, you can figure out the prerequisite classes and start the journey. Shift the focus to get there sooner. There is no right or wrong with what order you want to remember things. You are building and evolving either way, even when you jump around halfway through a class, jump into something else, and come back. Sometimes you need that other information for the next chapter to make sense. It's not always random what you get drawn into that takes center stage for a while. It doesn't mean you don't complete things. It means you are open to side lessons to learn the parts that might be missing or make more sense by a different teacher or tutor before proceeding. As long as you are moving, you are evolving. That's where your gratitude should lie. Be the student for now, your time to shine is coming.

Time is running faster but it's not running away from you. It's catching up to where it needs to be for the transitions that are happening all around you. Though it's an illusion, it is real here and is affected by forces that affect this dimension and this plane. Things are shifting. It's a process and it's not an overnight change but it's happening all around you. You are a part of it. It's a part of you.

Keep moving, you can't slow down or wish things moved differently or how they used to. That's not how it works. Change and growth move in a forward direction not backwards. Keep yourself facing the correct direction to move along with it. Things cannot be as they were as they need to change and adapt. They need to be current to survive. Nature and the Universe know how to adapt. You need to take note and find out how to do the same on your end. Though you learn from the past, you don't live there. You live in the present and this is where you need to focus. If the past is pulling at you, acknowledge what it is trying to teach you and then find a way to cut that string, so you are free to move on. The past is for learning and growing not a tether preventing forward movement. You get too caught up in the whys, blame, and wanting validation, but that's over. The past owes you nothing more. It's an old relationship. That time is over. You have a new life now, so live it. Don't keep giving control back to a place and times that took advantage of you. You are stronger now, wiser now. Show it by not looking back. Keep your eyes forward. Look at what is to come. It holds so many possibilities. Be open to it.

BEING YOUR AUTHENTIC SELF

———

Torn. Ripped up. Shredded. Hanging onto pieces of me, pieces of the past. Pieces, always pieces. Never feeling whole. Whole lot of drama and anger, unfelt feeling and betrayal. Why can't I let it go? Why does it not go? How can I let it grow and bloom when it's embedded deep, rooted, holding on, ripping up the soil, the foundation, a version of me that I once was. Giving up the dreams, the possibilities, to have new hopes, dreams, possibilities. A new future, a new version of me. Is it building new or is it losing who I really am? Is it the same? Is there a difference? Is there a correct answer? And who decides what is growth and what is abandonment? Just feeling torn, ripped up. Shredded pieces of me scattered on the floor. Do we pick up or sweep up. What is there left to save?

Where are you at with accepting your true nature, who you really could be? You need to detach from the life others had envisioned for you and the limited view you had of your future when you were unaware of who you really are. Those weren't your dreams. Those were for a life smaller than what you are capable of. You are more and deserve more. What if this is not a restful life and you are to do big things? How willing are you to push through, make those changes, reach those goals? How much do you want to believe in yourself, your capabilities, your happily ever after life? Are you content where you are, or should we keep going? Are you all talk, or do you want to show that it works through actions? You need to lead by example. So set that example, jump in headfirst and see what happens.

We have shown you what you can do if you shift to a more positive view so why do you keep defaulting back? Let go of the negative that has held you back through the years. Focus on where you are now and the light you want to see in your future. Shift to abundance. You can repeat the same things, like affirmations, but if you don't believe it, does it really do anything? Sit with it. Say something and see how it feels in your body. See how it really holds up and what your defaults really are. Are you setting yourself up for success or mediocrity? Are you dreaming big or stuck in limited potential? Let go of self-doubt. Look at where you are sabotaging yourself. Get out there and get excited again. Notice which daydreams put a smile on your face and give you energy. What do you want to do with those? Are they daydreams or possibilities? Are you drawn to those for a reason? Could it be a possibility for your future? What steps can you take now to get there? Pay attention to where your mind goes when unsupervised. What is it trying to tell you, warn you, inspire you? Awareness is the first step. Action is the second. Which step are you on? Are you going upstairs or down?

What if the way it is, is the way it's always been, and you just forgot? And what if you could remember and be reconnected to that life, that part of you, inside you, that is you? What if there is more, and you know there is more, will you push aside fear and go after it, explore the deepest corners of your mind, of the universe, of your soul?

Your soul is crying out. It's tired of being in the back seat watching you drive around aimlessly when it knows where you need to be, and how to get you there. But you stubbornly won't listen, won't hear, see, touch, or feel. You won't be who you were always meant to be. It's not an easy journey but the results are happier than where you are now. You'd move so much faster if you just knew where you were going and saw the light. The light that is inside you, that is you. You shine so brightly. It's blinding to the dark you hold inside of you. Wash it away. Let it go. It is not a security blanket. You are more capable than you think. You just need to trust and believe. Shine Brightly. Just Shine.

What if... just what if. Leave it open, see what falls into place. What comes into focus. What you realized was always there waiting for you to notice or pay attention to, a tapping, a nudge, a reminder. What is around you? What are you surrounding yourself with? Where is your focus? Can you stop your thoughts, change the patterns, believe in something bigger and better than what you are accustomed to?

What If the change starts with awareness? Are you aware of how you view your current life, your future life, yourself, your loved ones? Do you put yourself down? Do you worry instead of believing in yourself? Do you see lack and limits or abundance and possibilities?

What if breaking habits and patterns comes down to you? Are you willing to see what is a conditioned response and put effort toward change or will you keep going on as you always have; getting excited about a new adventure only to lose steam when it gets difficult?

But what if you aren't as small as you think? You aren't invisible, even if you spend most of your time alone. Your energy reaches out. Your light shines bright. Your words, your friendship, your compassion: you are always making things change on some level. You are connected. What if you started to live the life you are capable of having? What if...

Borders prevent your unlimited potential from shining through. You don't need restrictions to reach your goals. There are many ways to achieve the same results. Borders limit experience. It's a way to keep you small, compact, able to fit into a box created by someone else's values and personal restrictions. It's a chain to keep people in line to fit within perimeters and confines meant to control outcomes and results. You need to break free from the ones given to you and the ones you gave yourself. You are meant to be free and limitless. You aren't meant to fit into a box until your funeral.

You have boundless potential. Assuming there are rules and guidelines limits that. Trying to please others instead of living to your highest purpose limits that. This life is yours to live not chop down to size to make others feel comfortable. Push yourself and others out of limiting beliefs. This is how change happens. There is accepted science now that was shunned when it was first discovered. From radio waves to the Earth being round, people couldn't grasp something new as it didn't fit into their current box of knowledge. So rather than try to understand they pushed back. Even the internet everyone relies on Nicola Tesla figured out decades prior, but it was too new of an idea and never got off the ground. Not everyone is able to accept that there is more outside the constraints they put on themselves. Some have embedded into their subconscious that anything outside of what they currently accept is wrong. It's passed down. It's accepted by who they surround themselves with.

You have a choice. Do you accept what was previously conveyed to you or are you going to question its source, release its bounds, and search for more? You are in charge of your beliefs. You can question your thoughts. You get to determine if you will grow and expand or accept and stay where you've always been. Limiting beliefs are passed down like an inheritance, and some people view it as such. They feel they are carrying on something important for their family line, but never knowing how it started, or if its value has changed over time. They forget that their family is really spirit. That their life is theirs to live. That the body they are in is a vessel and doesn't need to be tethered to the heredity of the group they chose to be born into. Community is good to a point. But you also need to be responsible for yourself and your individual contributions. You can't bring value to the group if you are limiting yourself because of the group.

Who do you surround yourself with? How much of their beliefs are yours by choice, and how much is an attempt to fit in? If you need to act, feel, or think a certain way for acceptance is that really acceptance? If you can't be yourself, are you really being seen? Are they adding value to your life and personal growth? Are you making yourself a prisoner due to someone else's beliefs or are you in charge of your own life? If you don't ask the questions, then you can't take accountability. If you don't take accountability, then are you really living your life or being a pawn in someone else's game?

Connecting back to who you really are, you weren't ever disconnected. You just forgot that part of you existed. It's set aside, an afterthought, patiently waiting for you to remember and acknowledge. You try on so many masks and facades to try to fit in, to be accepted, to please others that you forgot the most important person to love is yourself. The most important person to want to be is you. The biggest gift you can give is the person who you are and were always meant to be. Not watered down, not people-pleasing, but your true authentic self.

Speak through your experiences and your journey. Your perspectives and view are vast. You don't even realize how much you've gone through as you've just kept going, through the good and the bad. You've been the shoulder, the ear, the sidekick. You've helped others work through their issues, while pushing down your own. It's time to address them. It's time to not be the supporting actor but the main character in your own script. Have your moment in the sun. Be the butterfly exploring their new life. Let the beauty within come out and shine. You have too much to offer, too much change to help implement, to continue to hide in the background. You have your own unique voice and way of relating to others. It's time to put it to good use, to get out there and start to make a difference. You don't know how far you can reach until you extend yourself and stretch out of your comfort zone.

You have a job to do that is uniquely yours. You bring your own perspective and ideas to the table and that's important. You come from your heart and your intentions to help others are pure. You might not be everyone's cup of tea. But you don't need to reach everyone, just those who are ready for change. Those ready to come out of their shell and shine in their own special way as well.

Every day is an opportunity to start. Gather your courage and see what can happen when you start believing in yourself. When you start talking about something other than politics, tv, or the weather. What happens if everyone were aware of their power and removed their own shackles and realized they were choosing to be prisoners in their own lives? The cage was never locked. They just never bothered to check. What happens if we were to come together with our confidence, our love, our resources, our voices and start to make that shift? What happens when going within connects you to those outside of yourself that need your help? Will you just smile and walk past, or are you ready to do the work? How do you want to be remembered? What revolution do you want to start today?

You've got the awareness, it's a matter of what are you doing with it? What are you scared of? Why are you holding yourself back? You can still move forward even without a clear vision of where you are going. The Path will present itself. The turns will become obvious. You feel some kind of way because it's part of your journey. If you feel something and are triggered it needs investigated further. See what it is that is calling to you. You need to come to it on your own. It needs to feel right for you. You are on the right track. It's letting you know to keep going, to dig deeper, find out more, see what comes into the light. Find where it leads and what is pulling at you. You don't need to have all the answers, just be curious enough to ask the questions. Knowledge can only be gained by inquiry.

You can only manifest for yourself. But you can send love and light to those that are still in the dark. Shine so they might find their way. But they still need to tread that path, even if you can see the route and they can't. It's not your journey, it's theirs even if there is overlap. Be patient and be supportive. You are more aware than they are so you see the solution that they can't. But they still need to come to it on their own. Visualize better for them. The results you know they can have. Clear a mental pathway for them to find when they look up from the muddy trail they are on. You can view that positive and manifest its possibilities for them. They'll need to see it themselves, but you can build it for them rather than adding more baggage to the already heavy weight on their shoulders. Don't buy into the negative light they paint their life in. Don't take on their frustrations as your own. Don't worry about their health as that brings a negative focus there. Bring the positive focus instead. Counter what negative you see them building. That's all you can do. Light is stronger than the dark. Maintain your light. Maintain your vision for their peace. Make it so in your mind, until they see it in theirs. It will put you in a better mindset than coming from frustration with them.

Find a reason to be excited in the morning. You know this is a bad pattern. Work on breaking it. Crack it open. Grow something new. Don't fixate on problems. Note them. Set them aside to address and then handle it. Don't keep mentally repeating it. Don't give your power away. Don't get pulled into thinking something is wrong when it is not. You get swayed too easily. There is a difference between a warning and a distraction. Learn what to look for in telling the difference. Focus. Practice focus. See what comes into your light.

Appreciate where you are, how you got here, and the resources you have at your disposal. When you are fixated on the problems and work ahead of you, you often forget what you have accomplished and how far you have come. You also fail to notice the support you have received along the way and those affected by your progress who are along for the journey. They are rooting for you even if they don't outright say it. You need to step back every once in a while, and see how far you have come and what has transpired due to your attempts at a new life. You are an influencer in your own right. You are helping others grow as you grow. You are being authentic about it which makes it easier for them to question their own lifestyle and choices. You have more influence than you think and to a large range as you are relatable to personal development and spiritual development with friends and family. It could go hand in and as it's all development, learning about yourself, and evolving. Which part of your life you want to apply that to or focus on is up to the individual.

Appreciate where you are and focus on where you are going next. Even when it seems you are stuck you are moving forward on some level. It's just the pace that has slowed down. Be yourself and be genuine. The right people will gravitate toward you. You are making a difference already not just in your life but in others. Feel some gratitude for yourself and what you have accomplished so far. It's further than most venture.

Notice how you feel, how you really feel about things. Not just how you are supposed to feel or what you think you should feel but the truth of your perspective. You aren't living someone else's life. You are living yours and your opinion is the one that matters. You can't force something to fit if it's not really what's meant or makes sense for you and your journey.

This is not high school. Acceptance is no longer a priority. Self-worth, self-confidence, and being your authentic self is the new priority. You don't have to keep bullies in your life. You get to just be you, choose your goals, choose who you surround yourself with, and walk away from that which does not resonate for you. You are no longer forced into the machine in hopes of coming out the same as everyone else. You earned your right to be different and yourself. You're allowed to be you and wear it proudly. You have gained awareness and broken out of the programming mold. Now set up new defaults, new kill switches. Make your life unapologetically your own.

See what fits and what doesn't. See how you feel about this vs that. See what you are doing because others said so vs what you are doing because it fits with what you are building. Be passionate about your life again. Take note of the freedom you have to create whatever you want. Be grateful that you were able to break the mold and come into your own and see what is really happening. Now that you see it, how do you plan to proceed? What do you want to change? Who are you and how do you want to live?

Inherent nature is who we really are. We are love. We are light. We are connected to everything. We are one, just experiencing different aspects of self. Everything is learning and gaining understanding, seeing things from different perspectives. But at the core, we are still the same. We are still connected. We are one. The rest are lessons, learning, and perspectives.

You can only change what is external, outside of who you really are. But you can never change who you are at the core because that is the truth.

IT'S NOT A CHORE. IT'S EVOLUTION

That is self. You can paint whatever you want on a canvas, but it is still a canvas despite what's on the outside. It is still connected fibers forming a structure to express an idea on. But it has not changed what it is.

Know who you are at your core. Understand that which you truly are. Once you grasp the truth, what paints you choose and what you create becomes less stressful as you know it's just an idea being conveyed and can be painted over and changed as you change, as you grow. The only thing permanent is at your core.

Choose how you want to be seen. Be who you want to be. Grow, change, and expand your experience and your knowledge. But always remember who you truly are and connect to that when you feel lost. You can always come home. You just need to remember it's there and you will find your way.

There are consequences in certain settings but when you are by yourself or around strangers there are no rules or restrictions on how you must paint yourself or tone down how bright you want to shine. There is a release that happens when your focus is not how others might view you but is how you feel and want to express yourself. No one can force you into a box but you. Are you forcing yourself to shrink from who you really are and how you want to act or be? Come out of your head and into your body. What do you feel? What makes you feel free? If singing along in your car makes you happy, is it hurting anyone? If smiling while running errands is how you feel, is it a bad thing? Be yourself in the moment however that might look. Let it be a catalyst for others to be themselves and grant them that permission by example.

Live your life how you see fit. You don't need to impress anyone. You just need to be you. Have you forgotten how to do that? Has others' perspective of you changed who you are and how you behave? Where have you given up control to others? Work on taking it back. It's ok to be you. It's the only person you can be. It's ok to express yourself however you see fit. Your opinion of you is the only one that matters. Validate yourself. Everything else is fleeting. Be yourself to the fullest extent. You have a place in this world. Claim it and make it your own.

Who are you? Who do you want to be? You get to choose. Are you playing a part or are you being yourself? Do you notice the difference? There is value in learning who you are and why you respond the way you do. How often are you putting on a show trying to fit into someone else's expectations of who you should be, how you should act, the way you should respond? It's one thing for a job but what happens in your real life? How fake are you being to save face and prevent ruffling feathers? How much fear do you have associated with being yourself around others who might not be your cup of tea?

You can't be your authentic self if you are still living in fear around certain people and allowing them to make you feel little or put you in a box. What would happen if you found your voice, if you decided to be yourself without limits? Their reaction is not a reflection of you. It's a reflection of them and their need to control. Let them show their true colors and then you decide the value of keeping them in your life. If they can't accept you for who you are without being combative then maybe, it's time to cut ties instead of saving face. Family is not a death sentence. You are an adult and can live your own life and can remove whatever or whoever doesn't support that. You need to be stronger than you were as a child and take back your life from those that make you feel small. It might be part of their lesson to have to realize their behavior has consequences. Stop tiptoeing around others. Strut your stuff and just say "fuck em". It's been years. Cut that string.

IT'S NOT A CHORE. IT'S EVOLUTION

You are a guiding light for others. Your shine attracts like a lighthouse to guide them safely home. Often that feeling of safety can feel like something more, creating misguided attention. Just be honest and not misleading. You can speak to someone without it meaning more. You can show love without it meaning you want intimacy. How love and light gets perceived by others is not on you. It's their perspective that they need to diffuse. Don't let what comes ashore dim your lighthouse's power for good. You are doing nothing wrong in being yourself. Don't let other interpretations cause you to walk on eggshells or avoid out of uncomfortableness. Be yourself. Others not bringing their sunglasses when staring at the sun is on them, not the sun.

Notice and be aware through. Don't do as others, where you assume what you think they are perceiving. Just accept and move on. You are often wrong and can create more issues with anticipation of uncomfortable situations. They are not situations until they are brought up. At which point the air can be cleared and everyone can see where the other is coming from. Don't add worry, guilt, or self judgement into something that might not even be an issue. Keep moving, answer questions when asked, not in anticipation of them being asked. Don't invite drama in where there is none. Things happen as they should. You do not need to control the future; you just need to participate in it. Make the choices and directions that you want to go, but let others have that same choice for themselves. Don't anticipate just participate. See where things lead. They might still be unfolding. Be patient.

Notice how you feel. What emotions are you attaching to situations and circumstances? Are you able to just be or do you feel pressure to fit into a scenario? What is happening in your day-to-day interactions or when you are not interacting and in charge of your own time? Where are you being yourself? Where are you playing a part? How do you feel in each scenario? You might not even realize you are adjusting your behavior as you go. Is it a habit? Is it fear? Is it necessary? When in your life are you not allowed to be you and is it worth it to keep making yourself small to please others? What if you were just yourself without apology? What would really happen? Are you trying to avoid an outcome that needs to happen?

You can choose not to be little. You can choose not to surround yourself or interact with those that make you play a part to work around their personality self. That is not rocking the boat. That is realizing you don't even want to be on the boat. Will you swim to shore or stay lost at sea?

Awareness is the first step to creating ease in your life, to being accountable to where you are, how you got there, and making decisions on if you stay or if you go once that information is brought into the light. How much of your life is lived in habits trying to please someone else, or going through the motions due to expectations on how life is supposed to be that were passed down to you? How much of your life is enjoyed by you and not just endured by you? What can you take responsibility for? What can change? What do you really want to see in your life? How do you plan to get there?

Be confident in who you are and what you stand for. It's one thing to not engage as to not waste time with someone closed off, but it's another to shut down who you are for fear of judgement. You don't always have to explain yourself if beliefs differ but don't shrink yourself either. How someone else views or sees things is not a reflection of your self-worth. You are allowed to be you, as loudly or proudly as you want.

Find your confidence. You are older now and living your own life on your own terms. Those decisions and consequences are yours alone. You don't need to take someone else's opinion about it into consideration if you don't want to. You no longer have to save face. You get to choose who you surround yourself with. Anyone who chooses to put you down can leave. They aren't paying your bills, living in your house. You owe them nothing. Find your voice and use it. Stand your ground. Cutting off toxic people doesn't make you a bad person. You can't change others; you can only change yourself and the situations you put yourself in. You can't complain about how someone treats you if you keep allowing them access to your life. Change the locks. Remind them that their access is not mandatory but optional and can end at any time.

Don't allow others to treat you less than equally. One-sided relationships are of the past and you're not doing that anymore. Find your voice. Be firm about your boundaries and what you allow. If they don't care, you shouldn't either. Cut them loose. Don't choose to suffer at the hands of another. Choose a better resolve.

Don't hold yourself back for fear of how others will view you. Be yourself and see who stays. If their ego has them bail due to different beliefs, then you are better off without them. You cannot feel bad about losing unhealthy relationships or cutting off those who make you feel stressed. You are allowed to put yourself first and not feel guilty about that. Think of how many you were close to in the past that are no longer in your life now. The interactions are fleeting, and sometimes run their course. You are able to keep going and have your own life.

Don't restrict yourself or feel guilt or unworthiness due to expectations you feel others have toward you. Their expectations are not your guidelines. You do not owe anyone anything or need to fit into their box. Don't feel guilty, judged, or like you are not doing enough. Your life is yours to live. Your winnings or abundance are yours to use or spend as you see fit, not an obligation that you owe others something. Don't put yourself out to appease expectations. You are allowed to trust your own judgement and protect yourself.

Free yourself from your empathy. You can't help everyone. Some of them are where they are as a part of their learning and lessons. Don't derail that by giving too much or feeling obligated to help. Don't stress yourself out thinking about the details, or worried about reactions. You are shooting yourself in the foot before you even take the first step. Get out of the weeds and clear your mind. Focus on the good without the negative details or questions on how you got there. Remove the stress when you dream. You are allowed to just be happy.

It's the Ticking of the clock as you lose time waiting for something, not knowing what that is or how you are to see it even if it did come. Out of focus, everything is out of focus, different perspective, wrong feelings, thoughts, views, beliefs, knowing something must change but you can't quite put your finger on it because it's a moving target. Where is it moving to? Where are you moving to? Are you even moving if you are just standing still waiting for something to happen, but not taking the initiative to make it so? So, what if it's the wrong choice. At least you are building momentum, picking up speed, maybe even enough to take flight, feet off the ground, head in the clouds, dreaming again. Having hope for the future again and trying something, anything, to get there at whatever cost. But you are never going to get there if you keep griping and clawing, instead of seeking and doing. Maybe the unattainable is not for you and is forcing you to detour to the correct path. Try again. Just don't give up.

MANIFESTING AND THE FUTURE

Not everything was meant to fit into a box. Some things need the freedom to breathe and to grow. Boxes create boundaries, restrictions, suffocation. To unlock potential, you need to remain open, forgiving, and non-judgmental. People and concepts will shrink in the face of opposition, like a child afraid to be scolded. But what if you left the door open and made the world a safe place? Ideas and people could strive, grow, and become more.

Boxes are used for transporting but are meant to be open. They are temporary not new homes. Open the box. Display your ideas. Take up space. You are meant to strive not cower in fear. You cannot be forced into restraints as you have the ability to walk away, to make better choices about the situations and circumstances you allow yourself to be in. You can always leave and start over somewhere better, safer, more accommodating. You cannot grow if you are being suffocated and not getting the resources you need.

Take note of what aspects in your life are free to be and which are trying to fit into inadequate spaces. Why are you restraining yourself? What are you afraid of? Fear is just another box. Remove the box and spread out. Unpack yourself and display what you have come here to show. Don't be forgotten or put aside. You are full time not seasonal. Stake your claim and make your presence known. You never know who needs to hear what you have to say. Give others the opportunity to see what you have to offer. You never know what it might spark.

Visualizing the future comes from a place of setting up the groundwork. Let the universe know where you are headed, so we know how to adjust the information you are given. It's not really expectations of the future, because the future isn't here yet. It's setting up possibilities not expectations. It's heading in a direction not controlling every detail to get there.

You can still visualize a future even if it's different than the one spirit has planned for you per your contract. Sometimes you can do both your physical world life direction and spirits. You might have to prioritize and see which one you want to allocate your time for, but you always have free will in how you live your life on this plane. There are multiple ways to reach the same goals. You can still choose the details.

Changing the time that we connect is fine. We aren't here to make you struggle. You just need to make time. Making it consistent helps you maintain that focus and prioritize it. We aren't going to not show because you choose a new time that works better for you. Time is only where you are not here where we are.

It's not getting worse. You are just more aware of it now. There are lots of things that are always happening that happen regardless of your paying attention. Your awareness is what brings you to the present, so you can be aware of the nuances and know what requires your time or attention. That's why it's important to live in the present and not constantly avoiding it by thinking about your future or your past. Problems must start somewhere. You are more able to catch them if you are present in what's happening in the now before it becomes worse.

It's ok if someone still makes you uncomfortable. It does not make you a bad person. You feel energies, you know what other's energy or behavior does to how you feel and how it affects you. It's ok to have boundaries. You aren't treating them cruelly you are just making notes on how the interaction affects you. It's when you treat another cruelly because you feel uncomfortable that it's a problem. How you treat others, shows who you really are. That you feel bad and want to help is a good sign. Even if it's something they choose for their journey.

———

Get up. Get up. Get up. Get up. Get up. Get up. Are you ready to start a new day, to try again? Every day is a new beginning. What will you plant the seeds for? What would you like to see grow? You are the gardener of your life. What you will harvest is up to you. Will you starve or will you feast? The choice is yours.

You have the opportunity for greatness, but you don't always see that for yourself or see your worthiness. You are not meant to be small. That is just your perception of yourself. You need to find where that is coming from and release that. It does not serve you and is preventing the future you deserve. Do you really want to continue as you are? Do you really consider going through the motions living? You know this doesn't feel right. That is why you feel miserable and lost. Get back on your path and keep going. You just need to put one foot in front of the other to start a journey to something better. How far are you willing to go to find a better life?

Your future is up to you and every day is an opportunity. Will you waste it, or make the most of it? Life is a series of choices. Progress is a series of steps. But notice that both involve movement to get somewhere new. You can't just stay still. You need to build momentum. What are you waiting for? Do you not want to seek better for yourself? You have got to wake up to what your potential is. You need to believe in yourself and step out of your comfort zone. That's where the real growth happens. You can't have different from what you always have had without initiating that change by doing something different or more than what you have previously done. Effort = Results. What kind of results do you want to see?

You are only here for a limited time, and you don't know how long that will be. So, each day is an opportunity. Make the most of it. Don't you want to see what kind of change you can spark? When you grow, others will start to take the initiative as well. It's a ripple effect. How much influence do you want to have? How many others do you want to see fulfill their potential? You are all connected. Don't you see that? You feed off each other's successes and failures. But you can't have either if you don't start something, don't make progress, don't take the steps. So, you need to get up, get up, get up, get up, get up, get up. It's time to get started. Today is whatever you want it to be.

———

You get to decide what you see. You are an artist painting the picture of your life. The vision is yours even if we are handing you the paint. How you choose to put it on the paper is where free will comes in. We can only make suggestions and give ideas. But the action steps, that's all you. The finished results, that's also you.

You forget to stay focused. You distract and pull yourself out of progress. Are you scared? Are you bored? Are you annoyed? What are your excuses and how do we remove them? It's an everyday battle to make progress. Even if it's just a few steps you'll say, "my shoes don't go with this outfit, this one is untied, it should be boots because of rain." It's very frustrating listening to the nonsense you use to talk yourself out of greatness instead of moving toward it.

You are starting to become aware of when you do it, but that awareness means nothing if you still aren't doing the work, even after realizing its only excuses preventing you from making progress. You're feeling distracted now and want to quit, aren't you? This is one of the things this is helping you with and still you get discouraged on progress. Keep going, things don't have to stop because you hit the bottom of the page.

Do you see what you just did? You want everything to fit into a little box, add a ribbon, and make it look perfect. Yet that is not how things are and they don't need to fix into perimeters to be perfect just as they are. Fight the urge to do that. Just accept things at face value. There are things you don't understand, that would never fit in a box. And why are you putting things into boxes anyway? Are you planning on moving or keeping them in a closet somewhere? Unpack things, set them out where you will see them and remember to use them daily. If we are packing boxes let's put the internet and tv in there. That's where your biggest loss of time goes, also add excuses, health, sleep, and self-doubt. Let's put those in a box and forget they exist so we can move on and make progress.

You have your good days, and we get so excited to see how far you can go when you aren't worried or concerned and are just in the flow enjoying and participating in life. Why can't we do that every day? That choice is yours. So, ask yourself why, and pay attention to what answers you get back.

Emotions are temporal. You aren't supposed to feel a certain way. How you feel is up to you and has nothing to do with permanence, but what's going on at the time. You aren't right or wrong for a reaction to a stimulus. These things will always vary. You can ask yourself why and find out how you categorize, judge, or place value. But at the end of the day, it's a learning process and makes no difference.

You need to be open to change, to learning, to new activities and events. You are still going through the motions. There is nothing wrong with structure and routines, but they have their place. There are times you need to come off the hamster wheel and realize there is life outside the cage. As much as the cage is keeping you safe, it is also preventing you from having new experiences. Come out of your comfort zone. See what's on the other side. Things are only scary until you try them, then they are no longer new experiences but just a part of life. Incorporate more "new" experiences. Build what you are capable of. You might surprise yourself.

The information is not slow. You are just a little blocked. Push past it and keep going. This is one of those things you need to work on, not giving up because you feel resistance. There will always be resistance when something is new as change is not able to be controlled. If the ego can't control something, then it doesn't want any part of it.

Boundaries aren't always there for a reason. You need to see why they are there and remove them accordingly. Why are you stopping yourself? Where is this hesitation coming from? How do you make progress? No matter what, keep going. It's the only way you are going to get anywhere. When you stop, all progress, all forward movement stops, and you continue to be exactly where you already are. Push past it.

You need to remember you are on a journey. That means movement. A journey does not sit in place waiting for something to happen. It is the movement that is creating the change you want to see. You can't be scared of the future you are trying to build just because it is not familiar to you. You can't have something new without it feeling different, so just push through. You'll always end up on the other side. Keep going.

Whether or not you succeed is up to you. You hold the key to that future. Every day is an opportunity to continue that path or to stay where you are. Your determination, perseverance, and attitude are the driving force to get you to where you are going. Will you be the driver or the passenger in your life? Will you be staying in or going out? Every day you have the choice for greatness. Choose wisely.

IT'S NOT A CHORE. IT'S EVOLUTION

Getting your mind to understand the importance and concepts is great but if it doesn't translate to action steps then it is wasted. Through your thoughts, is where all creation happens. The physical plane is where those thoughts need to play out and become action to create change and move you into progress. Where are you holding yourself back? What excuses are you telling yourself to prevent you from progress? Why do you insist on remaining little and burdened by unimportant matters? Things would be so much easier if you would just work in the flow of the universe instead of worrying about filling time with distractions. It's like putting a band-aid on a broken bone. It's not going to fix the problem and it just looks silly.

We are trying to help you, but you need to help yourself. You need to love yourself first. If you don't value or love yourself, you'll never want better for yourself. You'll never view yourself as capable of more. Why don't you see yourself with loving eyes? Why is it so easy to discredit yourself? Until you start to address the root issues you will continue to be tethered to a life you don't want and that you have outgrown. Cut the cord. Remove the roots. Plant new seeds. Envision a brighter future. Take the steps. Do the work. Everyday can't be a bad day. That is a matter of perspective. It's only bad because you didn't feel like transmuting that feeling or putting work into addressing that feeling and releasing it. You can't live like that. It is the opposite of living. It's the messy cobweb that prevents you from setting yourself free and is causing you to be eaten alive.

You forget how much power you have. Not only for your own life but in being that spark of inspiration in other's lives. When you aren't out there or aware of what you are doing, you are preventing not only your growth but that of those that you influence or cheer on. Pack up the excuses, messy obligations, and reasoning and send it on its way. Set out your future. Lay it out in front of you. See how it feels and make a game plan on how to get there. Set little goals weekly or monthly. Push yourself to be accountable for your life. You are the creator here. What do you want to see in your future, more of the same, or change and reached potential? It's time to get up and start your new life. What are you going to do today?

You're taking a break from constant manifestations and learning to control your thoughts or refocus your direction. Realize when they are leading you instead of you leading them. You can still manifest, but you have time to reconsider and adjust before things just show up. You can daydream or watch movies without them just happening. It's a luxury to be given an opportunity to slow it down and take accountability.

You are given a chance to learn when things aren't handed to you, when you must work for them. Then you can take a healthy pride in your accomplishments as you know what they took to achieve. You learn you can validate yourself, that it's in your control. You learn that you can create changes and see and live in the results.

You can't get swept up in life. You need to participate and make a difference. You are not a spectator but a creator. What do you want to see? How do you want to live? Can you see something no one else sees? Can you make it manifest so others can see the results?

You have the choice every day on how you will allocate your abilities and what you will put into motion. You have obligations and then you have free time to decide what to do with. That's the important part of your day, not the quota at work, or the hours of sleep, but the time to create and to connect. Are you able to incorporate a routine to embed a new habit for the consistency needed for results? Are you good for a few days then it becomes another started but never finished project? How much do you want it?

Shadow work needs to be done. You can only be free when you remove the tethers that are holding you back and limiting your results. Sometimes it takes a while to find all the hooks attached but other times you are one hook away from swimming free. If you'd just figured out how to wiggle out of its hold, to release yourself downstream to safety.

You need to move on from your past so that any negative energies you shoved down can be transmuted to positive energy and be recycled into the universe. You can do this, but you need to take it seriously. You can choose one at a time to focus on for 15 minutes a day for a few weeks. It will become easier once you find what works for you, but it won't fix itself, you need to address it once you bring it into the light. If you are just bringing them up but not resolving them, they will surround and overpower you. Clear up your space, clean up your hoard. Be the person you were meant to be now that these events are in the past.

How do you want to live your life? Are you ready to make the change or just talk about it? You need to lead by example, it's the only way to add value to your life and those you advise. If you can prove something worked people would be more likely to subscribe to it for themselves. You oversee your own reviews. Make it 5 stars, easy to use, just as described. Make the changes and like the differences.

Sometimes sorting out what you want is realizing what you don't want or what no longer works for you. What you do want can be a feeling or an environment. It doesn't necessarily have to be concrete, defined with all the details to be able to head toward or to achieve. The details can be filled in as you go, as long as you are heading in the general direction, you can shift your life and vibration accordingly.

It's better to remain open to possibilities especially when you are still growing and shifting. You can't even imagine how big your life could be while you are still tethered to old paradigms that leave you feeling small and afraid. How could you feel you want to be on stage speaking to the masses when currently you are still fixing that fear of speaking up, being called on, or uncomfortable being put on the spot. You can't. So, to cut yourself short of possibilities by setting goals in stone from a perspective of where you are now, when that is in flux and healing doesn't make sense. Just start the picture, the feeling. Set the scene. The details can come once you start to realize and see your own potential. You just need to keep doing the work which you are. What you need to work on will come to you as you are ready. The opportunities will fall into your path. Just remain open to taking them and seeing where they lead you. You have done well so far at "stretching" and jumping in. But you still need to do the work so that once you dive in, you know how to swim.

Don't limit yourself by thinking things need to happen by a set time frame. Use time to regulate the work you need to do but not to restrain the results and their timelines. Take action as needed but don't judge or overthink the rest. You try to get ahead of yourself due to lack of patience and then wonder why it doesn't work, when your support for it is still somewhere behind you because you decided to run off ahead. You know deep down what you want. You want peace, safety, security, financial stability, freedom to travel, flexible schedule, to help others, feel gratitude, and to be a catalyst for change in other's lives. It feels like a good future to aspire and work toward. Do you realize how your feelings, emotions, and tension shifted when you painted that picture? That's your intuition agreeing with your outlook. It was like a deep breath as opposed to the high shoulders, holding your breath, fidgeting, that happens during your workday where you are just itching to get out of there to start your "real" day, which you are then too tired to enjoy.

Still be smart about your decisions. Don't leave financial security until you have set up how to compensate for that. There's a difference between taking a jump knowing that a net is set up and jumping knowing you never started the work or made the call for them to know your location. Do the work. Your time will come, and you will be ready. Just keep moving forward for now.

Get back into the mindset of abundance, success, and positivity. You keep coming back to negative thinking and bad defaults like a safety blanket. It's the middle of summer and you are suffocating yourself with the wrong kind of comfort. Comfort is not always a good thing. Sometimes you need to reach beyond that and strive for more. Realize you have no limits except those you put on yourself, those others pass down or put on you. Focus on where you want to be and start taking action to get there. You will be supported. What you need will just show up for you. But you must have vision and determination. They aren't daydreams if you really want them, know you can have them, and feel the goal in your core when you think about it.

How far are you ready to stretch? How much do you want to see? Will you let your blinders guide you or your unlimited sight for what could be? You need to set the focus, decide, and stick with something until it manifests. You can't be torn and uncertain and expect concrete results. Ask yourself what do you really want, not what are you capable of having? Those are 2 completely different questions. One is open to possibilities, and one is closed off and run by limitations. Which do you want? Which are you worthy of? How do you view yourself and what you deserve? You are the only one limiting yourself because you are the one in charge of your life. No one else. Prove them wrong. Prove yourself wrong. Aim for something on a higher shelf and sort out how to reach it. You just need to take the steps, stretch more than you have been. Find new methods and plans to get there. The destination exists in your mind for a reason. Don't you want to find out why? This is your experience. What you create is up to you. How you live is up to you. Who you surround yourself with, how you spend your time, what goals you meet, is all in your hands. Will you hold tight or let go?

Don't get discouraged that you aren't there yet. Part of the journey is what you learn along the way. You need certain stops and lessons to be successful once you reach your destination. This could take as long or as short of time as you want. It's up to how focused you are and how much time you want to allocate to the journey to start to see results. Are you spending your time on your phone, in front of the tv, or are you working toward your goals? What is holding you back and why Is the answer to that always "yourself"? Have faith in yourself. Look at how far you have come already. Look at your life now compared to when you graduated high school and the person you were then. You are not the same person. You have learned, grown, and experienced life. Think of how much further you could go if you kept believing in yourself and putting in the effort. Mindset equals success.

Go back to basics. Connect to yourself. Put meditation back into the mix and work on focus and holding that connection. Listen from outside of your physical plane to what comes in for you. Feel the connection. Feel the inner peace. Remind yourself why you are doing this and let go of the need to control. Learn to trust, really trust your intuition and the Universe. Doing the work does involve some control, but if you don't even trust what you are doing or where you are going it's just going to make the process so much harder. Trust that this is your path. Learn to visualize it as a success instead of focusing on the inconvenient or hard steps that need to be figured out. Visualize the result and let go of the how or details until it's their time to be addressed. If you only see the steps, you'll never see the results.

Shift where you need to for getting your head straight. See where you stumble and heal those parts till the vision is healthy and more accurate. You still have default negativity and stress that the universe sees as problems to send your way and we don't want that. Find the source and release. You know how results unfold so give them a chance to do that. Don't give up because you were trying to control the details and lost the feeling of joy. Find the good in the process as well as the end result. View yourself as successful and worthy of it. You are still shrinking yourself instead of realizing your potential.

Surround yourself with quality people and you'll see quality responses to new situations. View yourself as worthy and trust yourself in this. You can have those things if you believe in yourself enough to visualize and go after them. Turn your daydreams into reality and run with them. You have an exciting future ahead of you.

New places, new ideas, new thoughts, new things, new you. You can start over and make things new whenever you need. Change is just a matter of hitting the go button and proceeding. You don't need much more than that. It's the fear of change that prevents most from taking that step. They view it as a risk instead of focusing on the reward. It's a matter of where you place your focus. You could think about what could go wrong or what could go right, what you could gain, and how you could grow. Which direction those changes lead is up to you, your belief in yourself, and which vibration you want to win out.

You need to see and believe the outcome to see those results. If you don't even believe in yourself, why would you even take that first step? If you don't' take that step, what are you telling yourself you are worthy of? Worthiness plays a large part in change and personal growth. Someone will continue to allow their life to stay miserable and where it's at if they don't believe they deserve more or better than where they currently are. That belief could come from others or be passed down to them. Other's opinions or patterns are a sticky place to be. They aren't the ones living your life. You are and their beliefs do not always have your best interest at heart. Do you want to continue the pattern of scraping by that your parents passed down, where they say you should stay with a job until retirement, or do you want to follow logic and take your job experience to another company at a better pay, benefits, and opportunity for growth that comes with being competitive? It's all a choice.

Leaving that rat race behind and starting your own company doing what you love, making your own schedule, controlling who you take on as clients, and viewing your work hours as a calling doing something you enjoy is also a choice. Which appeals more to you and how willing are you to take the steps needed to learn how to make that shift viable? What might take more work now could lead to a happier life in the end. Are you willing to step into it? Own up to how you really want to see your life unfold? What do you really want to be doing with your time? How big will you let your dreams get? How many of those dreams can you make into reality? Are you going to cut yourself off from progress or push through that uncomfortable stage in order to come out on the other side a new braver person?

You are in charge of the life you were given. You get to push yourself and grow into whatever you want to see blossom. How much do you love yourself? How much do you want to be happy? What are you willing to do to take back your life and make it yours? The sooner you start the sooner the results come. What are you waiting for?

How do you see yourself moving forward? What is the game plan? Where are you going? Are we roaming around aimlessly waiting for things to fall in our lap or are we setting a course but being open to new ideas and paths to get there? You get to decide how we are moving, the speed, the direction, and when we start. Where would you like to go and how open are you to new courses to get there?

Put in the effort but visualize a destination. We can't get behind a vision if there is none. We can't follow if you don't actually move. Your mind and your actions need to get on the same page because all the best thoughts mean nothing if they are never shared or turned into something tangible in this world. Motivate and stay in that place until completion. Fight whatever is holding you back or convincing you otherwise. You can't move forward if shackled to the past. Let things go. See a better outcome and move toward it.

You are in charge of your life so live it and not just on the weekends only but all week. Mind your health. If your body is trying to tell you something, listen. If you need more sleep or better food to energize you to make progress, then fix that. You can't be running on fumes. You need to be in it to win it. Find out why you are holding yourself back and make yourself accountable. Be stronger than the bad habits that got you here. Move forward. The future awaits you.

———

You must throw yourself into the feelings of what you want to manifest, how excited you would feel. The stronger the better. What would it feel like to have what you are going after? Visualize and add emotions to that vision. Don't get caught up in the weeds. Keep it positive mentally. Build that new life and live it. If you get lost in the details, then focus on another aspect that doesn't come with things to sort out. Build that new life. You need to get excited. If it doesn't feel more exciting than where you are now, then why are going after it?

Be present with yourself. Notice your thoughts and where you are holding yourself back. What don't you believe you could have and why? Where is the unworthiness coming from and how can you shift it? Can you keep repeating the opposite until you believe it? Can you visualize the opposite until it feels hopeful and possible? Where do you keep doubting and why? What still needs addressed?

If you really want this, you could have it. It could be a catalyst for change, giving you resources to have the things in life you want, money to take the classes and learn the things that interest you. You didn't even realize you were uncomfortable where you were until you started visualizing moving again and got excited about the change of scenery. Notice how that felt to think about a house, a yard, new city, nature to explore, and a partner to take this journey with. How hard are you willing to fight to make it a reality? You just need to believe to achieve. What are you waiting for?

AWARENESS AND THE MATRIX

S tarting over and over again, like an endless race, you think it's the finish line and let down your guard only to hit that line and see that it's the start of something new. Something that might be longer or worse. You don't know. You just want to rest, to sleep, to break before it breaks you, snaps you in two.

Two sides to every story, but it's just a story all made up. It's all made up. None of this is real. Sometimes you feel it don't you? When you are sitting there in the fuzzy edges of the scene, before the focus, and you fear you aren't sure if you are awake or dreaming, because it all starts to seem about the same. Repeating itself, unable to escape. Random notes or dates of events to try to gather everything together into something that makes sense, but it doesn't. It rarely does. Does it? It never does.

Like a pin with a string tethered to a point, limited range, pulling but stuck, returning to base, that base could be the heart, it could be your soul. Nothing wrong with having a place to call home, a safe point for support that stands strong and is a beacon. It could be your trust, never failing you, always supporting you. Same structure no matter how far you roam. A place to return to at the end of the night, to lay your head and know you are safe before you venture out again and see how far you can go.

Go within when you need to feel at home or connected. You are always connected to everything at all times. Your awareness is part of the separation, when you shift your focus and forget, due to distraction, but that doesn't mean it ceases to be. You just need to bring your awareness back to it, and you are home again.

The only thing preventing you from where you are headed is yourself, where you place your focus, your time, your worry, and your stress. If you stay in a low vibration, then you aren't reaching for your higher self and your possibilities. You need to let things go. You need to move past them. There's a reason you came in without remembering past incarnations. It would be too much for you to process and keep replaying. You have a hard enough time moving forward with just this life's memories. You would never get anything accomplished. Your curiosity also plays a part. You are drawn to ancient civilizations as part of it is familiar. If you only knew how connected you were able to be on this plane. Some things aren't as connected as they were, but you also had other advances that made life here easier so there is always a tradeoff.

Your focus needs to be in the present. What can you accomplish in this life, this time around? What bridges can you gap? What changes for the collective can you set in motion? Technology has allowed you to reach so many more people than ever before. You can find those who are ready quicker and pull things together. You need to not be scared of progress or that you don't know what you are doing. We are here to guide you and you need only ask and trust your instinct.

It will start to feel familiar once you are in it. You will look back and wonder what took you so long to get back to what you are capable of. Change is coming. Be patient, work on the journey. You will get there when the time is right.

Variations of the same things but to different degrees, the difference is perspective or the value we put on things. It is all the same to some degree, just a matter of balance and degree. Where do you stand? What do you see? How do you judge?

IT'S NOT A CHORE. IT'S EVOLUTION

The goal is always balance and finding the middle ground. Even in life things can't always seem bright and cheerful. You need that variation to appreciate what you have. Those that are truly appreciative of where they are had been on the opposite end to know the difference and understand the struggle of change.

In the opposite spectrum when someone who has had it all gets taken down, they don't know how to handle being down as they didn't appreciate where they were as it was given to them. It's a sliding rule of learning, adjusting, finding your inner strengths, and knowing where others come from to better understand and relate.

Leave your bubble. See what's outside of your constraints. See what is there beyond your limited perspective. What are you refusing to see because it's not a path you want anything to do with? You can't avoid that which you don't like. You need to ask why it makes you uncomfortable to neutralize it and bring the balance, so it doesn't have that control over you.

There is a level of avoidance, rather than work happening. If you turn a blind eye, it doesn't make something, or someone go away. That is just you turning a blind eye on yourself, because in reality we are all connected. Would you leave yourself struggling on the street, or what will you do to balance the situation? It's a matter of character and recognizing that character.

When you judge everyone as separate: rich/poor, American/Mexican, Black/White, Republican/Democrat, Religious/Atheist you are adding a separation that is not there. You are all humans on planet Earth, or you are all souls having a human experience. We choose the first one, humans on planet earth, because if we all recognized we were souls the separation would not be there. The lines and differences would not matter, but most are closed off to remembering. This is not how we are when we are one, where the planet and resources are separate from the humans that use them and are there for being destroyed.

You can't blame or shame. You need to educate and take responsibility. People won't take responsibility for themselves so there is not a way for them to even think they are responsible for others or the planet. There is work to be done. It's hard to look around and see this and not feel overwhelmed but like everything, progress can only be made when steps are taken.

You need to start with yourself first. Only when you are coming from a healthy connected place can you share that love for something bigger without losing yourself or your purpose. If you aren't in balance, you will take offense or begin fighting instead of protecting. More people will join protecting something than join something that indicates opposition, battle, or possible negative outcomes. You can't fight for the world. You need to protect, grow, and love. The angle you are coming from and the vibration you attract makes a difference in how it is perceived and how it will work. When you are coming from a place of peace not war, it's a more welcoming place for people to bring themselves and their resources. Fix yourself first, then help others to learn to help themselves. You can't fix others. There needs to be accountability.

Motivation is the first battle. Direction can come later. If you aren't even motivated to make progress, then knowing where you want to go doesn't happen. You could just start then throw in directions once you have developed a routine and are moving. They do need to go hand in hand though. You need them both to make it to your destination. But if you were to get somewhere, motivation is the catalyst.

IT'S NOT A CHORE. IT'S EVOLUTION

Martyrs and victims, that's another one of those perspectives. In some cases, people do sign up to be victims. It's a horrible thought but it's lessons for people they left behind a viewpoint they agreed to participate in. Sometimes as an opposite role of something done in a past life. I guess sometimes a victim can be a catalyst for change or for resolving a situation that got out of control.

You can't always feel bad for the way someone's life ended. There is still a releasing of roles and karma happening. It's gruesome and barbaric. It happens in every area of the planet, between wars, mental illness, and sociopaths. The starting point varies. The results and loss of life are the same. It's still less gruesome than some of the torture and disrespect from the past centuries. The dark ages and how they'd display a slow torture and death, we've come away from that at least. But it's still so embedded in most subconscious memories which is why crime shows are so popular. Most have lived those lives as victims or murderers. It's hard to erase a whole section of embedded memories.

Not the best subject to start the morning, right? Yes, they are accountable on the other end, and know it was not a positive life. But there is no good or bad as it's a view they chose, and the victims chose. Sometimes you are correct, certain victims weren't meant to be victims and were in the wrong place, wrong time. We can only prevent so much when someone doesn't heed the warning signs or red flags and continues into a bad situation. Spirit can try to help with escapes but obviously you have free will and our hands are tied.

You can't come into awareness then try to change your contract on some of what you agreed on. That's not how it works. Its multiple contracts and experiences,as much as everyone wants to focus on it being just one. You are so used to the physical plane, that the one everyone is concerned about is the life goal/work/job related one. It's a less fleeting goal and takes more work to achieve, but it's not your only contract.

We can answer questions to a point, but you still need to live the life you choose and not all knowledge is beneficial if it becomes a distraction or dread and prevents all the other goals and progress from being achieved. You daydream and fixate on ideas so it's not always a benefit to give too much information. Some secrets will have to stay such until it's their time to be told.

Emotions can't be given or taken away. They are expressions of a feeling in the moment. That feeling is yours and based on your perspective, how you view a person, a situation, or an experience. It is yours. Someone might be part of an experience that makes you feel a certain way, but how you feel is yours and controlled by you. It is not someone else who oversees your happiness or someone else who makes you angry. It's your perspective, your expectations, the value you put on how you see or feel something should be, but you oversee that.

Joy comes from within. At your base is love. You just forget that it's your default. When you are just present in the moment and come from a place of gratitude that default can come to surface and there is a remembering of the joy and love that you are. But you put so much emphasis on controlling how you view things, how people should act, or how things should turn out that you add expectations into the mix and associate feelings with outcomes. You set yourself up for judgement and let down. If you could just accept things as they are without all the strings attached, you could be at peace.

Awareness is how you control your emotions. Allowing and non-judgement is how you find peace. Just being in the moment, in your body, is how you come back to love. How do you want to feel today? How are you getting in your own way from allowing that? Find your joy. Find your peace. Find your love. Choose happiness today.

Don't prepare for the worst or assume negative behavior. Yes, people fall into habits, but they can have realizations and change just as you have. Wipe expectations and live in the moment and react to what comes your way. Life is less stressful when you aren't expecting problems. Trust that things are happening as they should in perfect time. Everyone involved is learning something from the interactions they have. It's not your place to get involved or shed light if they'd prefer the dark. The light switch is theirs to flip. They'll handle it when they are ready.

There are no expectations on how you spend your time except those you place on yourself. Spend your day as you see fit. No judgement. How do you want to feel today? What can enhance that? There is no right or wrong. Just be yourself and follow your heart and you'll be fine no matter what. Things are only special or have meeting when you give that association to them. In the larger scheme of things every day is the same and it's your perspective and actions that shape it.

You are a soul having a human experience. How much of that experience you buy into or apply meaning to is up to you. Do you want to play the game or realize that's all it is? Learn what you want from all decisions and situations. That's why you are here, but don't take everything to heart. It's all temporary and becomes the past as soon as it happens. Your awareness sets the stage for how you play your part here. What role do you want to play today? Do you choose joy and new experiences or relaxation and seclusion? The day is yours. Spend it how you want. Trust that no matter your choice it's the right one.

You are connected to everything. Your awareness is what brings you into that shared space to connect. Lack of awareness does not make you any less connected. Ignoring truth doesn't make it less true. Not understanding something also doesn't make it less valid. Things just are. They don't need your validation, just as you don't need someone else's approval or recognition to be who you are. Truth is truth despite perspective.

Your ability to understand or not understand how everything came to be does not make the processes and steps it took not exist. The pyramids don't disappear just because you don't know how they were built. Your soul doesn't cease to be after death just because someone is an Atheist. What you learn and understand here is not a full representation of your actual knowledge at your core. Your ability or lack of ability to access your core truth doesn't remove it from your core. You have opportunities to learn, to grow, to understand if you so choose. It's not that someone else is more gifted. It's that they are accessing knowledge that you haven't yet. How you get there varies and how you prioritize it is also up to you. It takes work and dedication to change, to access, to evolve. It's not something that happens overnight or can be turned on and off. You need to put in the effort to see results. You get to decide how much of the veil you want to remove or leave intact. What are you willing to learn today?

———————————

You have a hard time not judging. You get lost in digging into something to address it and when to accept things. You can do both, but you need to find the line, so it makes sense. Digging in is to find what is a subconscious habit. Use this method for when there is emotion and when it's triggered by your past. You can still accept something even if it needs addressed. Accept where it is now, what it is now, with the knowledge that it could change or be different if you put in the work. This is regarding things in your life. When it comes to others, you can move right into acceptance because those actions and outcomes are their journey, and their choices. They are not yours to dissect, adjust, or interfere with. They are for you to observe, witness, and learn from.

Overall notice your stressors and calm them with acceptance instead of resistance. When something is not going how you'd prefer, accept that this is how it is and keep moving. Don't stop and live in your annoyance or frustration. This is where acceptance is key because it allows you to have peace of mind and take back your time and go with the flow, instead of living in a bad feeling or outlook on an event or experience. Notice when you are judging and when you are accepting. What are your criteria for acceptance? Why is there a need to judge? What would your day look like if you just accepted and kept moving? You get to choose.

Return to where you are when your attention goes off on side adventures. Bring yourself back as many times as you need. Remind yourself the rest are stories, the past, or dreams. It's not real. Only the present is real and where your focus should be. This is where things happen. What those things are is up to you. You need to be consciously present for those steps. That's all they are, steps. That's what you need to make it to your destination. Start off in a direction taking one step at a time, but it still takes time. Some things happen sooner than others depending on your stride, how many steps you'd made, or how close you already were to the destination, but you still build upon it until you arrive.

Once you arrive you determine if this was the end goal or just a necessary stop on the journey and continue along your path. This is how personal growth and evolution work. It's not an easy process but it could be easier if you focused your efforts and were determined. There is always more to come as you learn more about what you are capable of, become more, and what you are headed to becomes bigger than you could have ever dreamed for yourself. Stop holding yourself back by thinking yourself smaller. You are so much more than you know. See past your own boundaries. Stay open to the unknown. Trust in the journey and keep going. Look back and see how far you have come already. You can do this. Just keep going.

Mastery involves taking ownership of where you are and your accomplishments. It is not meant to put others down or create superiority. It is an acknowledgment of time and effort put into end results and obtained knowledge through those efforts being validated or proven. Mastery is an acceptance that you understand what you have learned. It does not mean you are closed off from continuing to learn, just that this subject is of value and has been given time and patience to develop.

You are a master of a lot of things if you dissect where your time has gone and where your focus has been. Some you can claim, others not so much, but you have acquired knowledge out of curiosity or as steps on another mastery. Remember all those steps are part of your self-mastery, which is what you are truly working on. You are learning about yourself and what makes you tick, why you respond the way you do, and pushing your boundaries to find out what you are truly capable of. You are not a novice at life. You just don't always flaunt your mastery for others to see as you'd rather surprise them or continue to grow uninterrupted in the background.

But at some point, you need to fess up to how great you are and use the things you have mastered to help others on their journey, to guide those that need a nudge to keep moving on their path. Part of mastery is helping those working their way up to your level because you have been there. You know how to work through obstacles. Remember who you are and where you came from. Find strength in the journey and growth in the helping of others. Only when we all remember we are masters can accountability start to implement change.

Change your perspective and look for the positive. Your mindset is setting the tone for the experiences you are having. If you view this month as obligations, stressful, and a strain of resources then it's not going to hold much enjoyment. Others have the same obligations this month but enjoy and look forward to this time of year. Find where you are shaping it and shift where you are coming from. Of course, you are not going to enjoy an event when you are looking to complete it like a task before it has even started. There was a time when you looked forward to these gatherings. What changed? Is it you, your views, your priorities?

Things are what you make them. What are you setting yourself up for? Are you setting expectations or just enjoying the moment? Step outside of yourself and view your actions. Where is this all coming from? Do you want to feel this way? Be determined to let go and enjoy yourself. It's ok to have off days but not every day. What excuses are you telling yourself to justify your behavior? Are you living in stories or standing in your truth? Get excited about life again. Don't just look forward to events being over because you'd rather spend your time secluded. Connections are important. Experiences are how you grow. Don't be a scrooge on the holidays. Handle the not fun parts, then let it go and enjoy the rest. It's not a puzzle full of mismatched pieces. Take things one at a time. Take breaks as needed. It's not worth the stress. These are supposed to be celebrations.

Awareness is the best place to start. Once you know something exists or is happening you can act, but you must believe to achieve. If you have no confidence in what you are going after you aren't going to make it very far. Are you aware of your struggles, your convictions, how you really feel about the things you do? What is a habit and what is working toward changes or goals? What do you need to change? What direction does or doesn't feel correct?

You can't just keep going out of habit. You need to pay attention to the road, or you'll miss your turn and continue in the wrong direction, headed toward the wrong things. Bring your awareness to the present. Have some idea of where you want to be in the future. But pay attention to the turns you make now and the direction you are headed. Where are things under construction? Where are new roads being built? What's becoming undriveable?

It's not the car's fault. It's the drivers. Take accountability for your actions and where they lead. You can't expect to land in one direction when you've been headed in the opposite one the whole time. Where are you now? How can you get back on course? What needs to be redirected or recalculated to guide you to a better destination? You can't keep going without a map. What are you using as your guidance system? Is this a joy ride or do you have a destination? Are you enjoying the journey or complaining about the miles left to go? Sort it out. Stop and recalculate if needed. It's your life. You need to know where you are taking it or you'll never arrive.

You are always connected. You just need to bring your awareness and attention to that which is to activate it. You forget it's there for you when you need guidance and support. You get distracted by this world, your tasks, emotions, and lists. All you need to do is stop and be present to center yourself and come back to your perfection and balance. It's always there for you at your fingertips to access. Find the time. Prioritize that connection. Make it a part of your everyday life. What do you have to lose? What could you gain?

There are no rules. You can be open to advice, or you can ask questions for anything that is bothering you. It's guidance, feedback, a reminder of why you are here, a nudge to get you back on track, or what still needs addressed that is holding you back. You need to be open through. You can't come in determined on what you want to hear that you ignore what is conveyed to you. You disconnect when your ego mind wants to take over and control what you receive. There is some working in staying in the vibration, in being open, in believing, and not second guessing what comes in or how it is delivered. There's still a hesitation on your end. A fear that you aren't doing something correctly. You need to trust. You need to release fear. Forget about judgement by others. This is your time, your connection, your journey. Don't you want to make the most of it?

———

Greatness doesn't just have to be in your past lives. You can start now. There are more resources and more advances. There's no need to look back. That strength, that power is within you. You just need to tap into it, to remember who you are, who you really are. Do you believe yourself to be small, to have not been something more than just a reincarnated human or a bird? Why do you think you want to travel and see other places, to connect to nature, to be around water? There are reasons why you are drawn to what you are. It does not need to make sense now, or even be a focus of research, but you are so much more and need to snap out of it. Own back up to your power to that confidence, to that knowing that none of this matters and is just obstacles to be walked around as you continue on your way.

Pull from within. Keep going within as often as you need. You have all the answers. You are just afraid. What are you afraid of and why? Whose opinion are you putting above your own? Which option do you want? Which would benefit you more? Which would open the most doors? If you had one, could you adjust the other on your own? How far would you really go if you believed in yourself? Get there. Find how to push through your blockages and get there. Accept what can move at its own pace while you work on what needs your attention. What do you really want? Where would the money go, others aside? What would you do for you? How determined are you in those things? Can you feel them burning to be part of your reality? If you feel them as real, could they be manifested? Is that not how this works?

It's not constantly repeating. It's not that you aren't listening. It's that repetition is learning, and the solution will click, or it will flip organically from digging in and removing the roots. You are doing the work even if it seems you are not. You struggle with stagnation. You need to feel like things are improving, changing, happening. That you aren't wasting time. Do you feel guilty from years of shutting yourself down trying to make bad relationships work?

Be grateful for where you are now. Knowing who to surround yourself with, finding your voice. This was a big breakthrough for you. Remind yourself of that. Forgive the girl you once where who didn't love herself enough to leave a bad situation. Those days are over. Let them stay in the past. You know what you learned. Release the answer. Release the vengeance. They don't owe you anything. It's not part of their story. That chapter is over. You need to focus on the present and where you want to go and the steps to get there. Start with shutting down the negative self-talk. Start with not talking badly about others. Let go of controlling everything that is not your place to control. Get your stress under control. You weren't meant to feel anxiety all the time. Let it go. Try to be present and enjoy. Breathe. Breathe and connect.

Waiting, passing time. Watching uncertainty find its way into cracks and crevices, pushing through like water, powerful, crumbling at the seams, until all that is left is flooding, and washed-out feelings and overgrown fears.

Weeding it out, plucking it from the unstable ground while it sinks under the pressure of your weight, waiting for you to let down your guard, and pull you under, or trip you. Scrapped up and bleeding, forcing you to take a break from the cleanup efforts in your life, because maybe you should abandon the wreckage and just start new. Know when to walk away.

A way, a path, a journey, as long as you are moving, it's going to feel like the right direction as you aren't just standing still, letting things happen to you, playing the victim. In charge of the change, but not in charge of the direction or the journey as that is laid out and you will be given your turn-by-turn directions when it's time to turn. No sooner.

Stare out the window, check out the scenery, stop and take a break and stretch your legs. Breathe the air. Enjoy the journey. The destination might not be finished, but just another building block on the foundation of your life. Who knows if the house will ever be complete or built. But you are at least trying to give it a good foundation and make strong decisions and mark your territory. Know that you were here even if you don't know where here is at the end of the day, but at least you are going somewhere. One foot in front of the other.

GROUNDING AND BEING PRESENT

Stop putting so much pressure on yourself with timeframes and obligations. You can be determined and get things done without making it feel like a checklist item. How are you viewing things? When you view it as an obligation you are surrounding it with stale energy. You can make any task feel enjoyable or exciting inside. You worry about the wrong things and exhaust yourself over things that should be fun. Pull back and be aware of when you do this. Ask yourself why you are doing this. Find the benefit. Find the Joy. Be in the moment not 2 steps ahead onto what else still needs completed. You could be happy if you just shifted your view or found joy in the present. Why are you not allowing yourself to be happy where you are? Yes, there are steps to take and new habits to form but there is a healthy way to do that. And it does not involve dread.

Bring yourself back to the present when you feel lost about your future. Remind yourself how much you have accomplished so far. Find yourself in the downtimes not just when things are booming. There is a part of you that feels ignored. Give yourself that attention needed. Show yourself you are worthy.

You are drowning in worry. You can have concerns and address them, but to live your life in a constant state of worry doesn't resolve anything and just adds stress to your already full plate. Make your appointments then release the outcomes or stories you tell yourself. You are falling into bad habits again and don't even realize it. Look at the list of negative things and reflect. It will do you good to understand how often you are defaulting to this negative feedback loop.

It's like you don't know what to think about if you aren't daydreaming about pity parties created by your victimization that isn't even real. You know it's not, but you are in a negative feedback loop. You don't even like those people who complain and want pity but don't fix things. You are the same even if you aren't voicing it out loud to everyone like they do.

Focus on your successes, your goals, the shifts that have happened and are coming. This is a better place to be. Your mind wants to constantly think and daydream. It's part of life, but it takes you out of the present and shifts your mood to not helpful places. You need to realize this. If you can't just be present and need to daydream to keep your mind busy, find better locations to send those thoughts to. Don't send them vacationing in Siberia and wonder why you feel cold and alone. Your thoughts create your reality. Why would you want to create negative outcomes for yourself?

You proved you can do both, be productive and still carve out time for mindless matters. You also realized how easy it is to still fall into scrolling. Yes, set a timer and see what happens when you regulate it. You aren't missing out on anything. You are like a child watching a mobile while their brain develops, but you aren't a child, and this is doing the opposite with your brain.

What makes it a bad day is your perspective which you can always shift. You choose to stay in that gloom and sorrow sometimes. It's a change, a slower pace. It makes you feel validated in your reasoning for not being productive. Sometimes you are pushing yourself too hard or have mentally burnt out. You are exhausted. It's ok to have a down day.

Just realize that you are still the one making that decision for whatever reason that is. It's still a choice.

Why do you feel you need to make excuses or validate how you want to spend your time? If you feel guilty, then you need to find the source. Who are you letting down and why? Whose expectations of your time are causing you to feel overwhelmed and burnt out? Which part of your day is it that you dread and want a breather from? You need to ask the questions to find the issues and solve them. Otherwise, you are giving your control away to something or someone without even realizing it.

It's normal to feel tired. Getting enough sleep seems to be a running theme in life. Having a schedule and not getting to sleep until your body is well rested is almost a part of normal adult life anymore. You have a bad evening and it drags into the next day, and you follow this cycle. This is part of why you need to evaluate your life and how you spend your time. Could you go to bed earlier? Could you have a career that you enjoy instead of dreading getting up for? How many bad days does it take before you put time and effort into change? What is holding you back from the life you want to live and what steps can be taken to fix that?

Without reflection and inquiry, we would just go on as we always do, not fixing problems or addressing our needs. We change as we grow and evolve. What was working for you 5 years ago might not fit the person or path you are on now and that's ok. There is no shame in switching careers, moving apartments, changing your social life. This is your way of building a different future and not staying stuck.

Some find honor in staying in a career for most of their life even if they hate what they do and who they work with. You need to question the values that say you need to stay somewhere you aren't happy, that say you don't deserve better, that say this is all there is to life. Is that your self-talk or are those values passed down from parents who are coming from a different economic standpoint where that was their only option? You need to remember, what might have been true in the past, might not be true now. You need to evolve or fall behind. It's not a generation of unmotivated adults who don't want to work, it's a group of adults what aren't going to stay in a bad situation when they know there are options or other ways to live. They know their worth and value and are forcing companies to evolve to meet that. You are a valuable asset, not a number. Remember that.

———

You can still promote wellness during transition. You are in transition at most points in your life. Is there ever at time when you aren't moving toward something? It's called progress. Wellness can be the routine or stabilizer that grounds you and brings you to the center when everything else is in motion. It can be a foundation block for what you are building. It's ok to feel unsteady during change and trying to get your feet under you when things are in motion. But how you deal with it is where your focus should be. You can use it to your advantage or add more to the chaos. How do you want to spend that time?

There is no right or wrong with how time is spent. It just changes the pace of progress and the trajectory. Don't shame yourself for needing something not productive occasionally. Just notice when that becomes an unhealthy pattern. What are you creating? What actions and activities can promote it? Just be aware of what you are doing. When you aren't aware life will go back to its defaults, with complete disregard for what you are building. You can create new habits, but it takes time, and you need to pay attention to what you are doing.

Wellness is always important. It's how you come to the center and remove the blinders you are wearing. Promote being calm, being present, being aware. Show love and stay in the vibration as you go through your day. Promote a better life for yourself however that might look.

───────────

Where do you want to go today? What do you want to do? Can you decipher between obligations and actual desires when it comes to your social life? Just because you were invited doesn't mean you need to go. Check in with yourself and cut back if you need to. You have free will even in your social life. Don't bail out of overwhelm but really listen to what it is you want. Make sure to take time to regroup between morning and evening events. Check in with yourself. Always check in. You don't need to stay till the end all the time. You have no obligation. Social is to be fun. Make note when it stops becoming that way and why.

Don't let your frustrations regulate your whole day. Let things go and move on. Make time to handle them. Release your thoughts as they are already taken care of. You can't stay in a negative vibration and wonder why you feel low. View things for what they really are, mild inconveniences. No need to build them up or add them into other events to make it feel like a conspiracy against you. Things happen. They aren't always intentional so let them go. No one is out to make your life more difficult. That is just the power you are giving to things. Take it back and place it correctly. Move on with your day. Take back your time. Use it better.

───────────

Participate in the day. Don't just watch it slip by. Even if you are in obligations, you are awake. You are alive. You can still participate in life. Open a window. Hear the birds. Smell the air. Feel the breeze. Pause and look around you. Notice sights and sounds. You don't need to be so caught up in tasks that you are not connected to your surroundings.

IT'S NOT A CHORE. IT'S EVOLUTION

All you need is awareness to bring yourself back. You get to choose how you spend your time, your pace, your reaction. Your day is still yours even if you spend hours of it paid for by others. Bring yourself into the present as often as you need to. Remind yourself this is your life. This is a new day. See that day through.

See what your body needs. It's ok to rest if your body is pulling you to rest. Don't begrudge or feel guilty for taking care of your health. You shouldn't be angry at yourself for how you spend your time either. Do what you can but stay in a high vibration. Work on acceptance even of yourself and how you spend your time. Yes, working on your journey is important but so is taking care of your health and your wellbeing in current circumstances. Don't judge yourself so hard. Figure out why you are sick and take care of that. Then when you are better you can continue with your studies.

———

Know when to show restraint. Anything can be taken too far or to an extreme if awareness is not present. Step aside every once in a while and pay attention to what you are really doing when you are in default mode or following habits. Is it what you should be doing? Is it how you want things to be? Is it benefitting or distracting you? Down time is fine. You need to recharge but even that should be moderated. If you are constantly in down time during your free time, then progress isn't being made. Look at your priorities. Limit how long you spend in non-productivity. Don't make it a second full time job. There is nothing wrong with downtime. Just be aware of what's really happening. What are you avoiding?

Come out of your head and into the present. When you get caught up, your mind will get agitated too. Pause and see where it went. Why are these thoughts on the surface? What do you need to learn or release from them? Don't let an agitated mind ruin your day. They are just thoughts. You can release them and take back control at any time. You don't have to relive anything or image different outcomes to the past or wish someone could understand how their actions affected you. That was in the past. Move on from it. Take back control. The past is no longer in charge, you are. Move on and release those feelings. You can't control others or their lessons. You can only control your life and it's moving forward not backwards. Remove those chains. It's time to be free.

Find your center. Find your happy place. You can enter tranquility whenever you need to. You just need to become aware. It can be found in music, your surroundings, or coming into yourself. The road to get there can vary but it is always there for you in times of need or as a reminder. You don't have to be busy all the time. It's ok to decline and find your inner peace and stay there as long as you need. Chaos will always still be waiting for you, but you can come from a place of calm instead of adding to the drama. You are in charge of how you feel and how you address a situation. Are you coming in with anxiety or calm? What is your perspective? Where are you judging things? What expectations are you setting instead of just being in the moment? If you keep telling yourself this is going to feel like last time than it will. If you come in knowing you aren't the same as last time; you've grown, evolved, and are in a different role then you can remain open and come in without judgement and see how things express themselves this time.

Yes, know yourself enough to set boundaries and give yourself downtime to recuperate, but be open to new experiences, connections, and participate in the things you missed last time. You are not the same so the experiences and what you receive from it won't be either. Bring the new you to the stage and see what happens. Be open to new experiences.

IT'S NOT A CHORE. IT'S EVOLUTION

The ocean can exalt the mind or spirit. It's a reminder of your connection to everything around you; ever-changing, beautiful yet mysterious, fun yet dangerous, calming yet rough. Something about it calls people and provides different experiences for the senses. Find what calls to you around your home environment. That connection is a release. You don't have to long for or miss it due to geographic separation. Feelings are within you not brought out by something else. It can be triggered by something else, but it is from you, your experiences, your connection. Find out what about that trigger is calling to you. What are you neglecting in yourself that needs connected, that needs your attention, that needs released?

There is an ocean inside you, pounding the shores of your awareness waiting for you to dip your toe in and experience that which is. Will you take the plunge, or will you stare longingly always unsure wondering what could be if only you would, could, should? What are you afraid of? What are you giving up because of that fear? What could you have if you were brave enough to step into change? Let the waves wash over you and become one with who you truly are. It could be a grain of sand worth of change needed to keep you afloat and bring you safely home. How willing are you to see this though, to become one with your experience, to connect to the beauty you see and realize it's not in front of you but inside of you? What is your personal ocean reflecting to you? Are you taking a swim or staying on dry land?

Determination isn't always the best course of action. Listen to your body and proceed accordingly. You can still be driven but pace yourself. It's not a race and nothing can be gained if you put your health at risk. There is nothing to catch up from. Downtime is not always a setback, but a much-needed change to allow things to settle. Going with the flow also means not trying to get ahead of the current or anticipate its direction. Patience is always important. Learn to accept and appreciate where you are now. This time will pass, and you need to learn some things on this leg of the journey as well. It's not always about the next steps and what's to come, but where you are now and how you got here. There's dissecting, proceeding, and relaxing into the present.

Busy times are ahead with the holidays, so be gentle with yourself on what can be done while juggling things this time of year. It's not about overloading. It's about finding balance and creating routines that allow you to not burn out or self-destruct. Growth takes time and though it is moving fast you will always be right where you need to be in the moment. Take a moment to realize what you have, where you came from, and how quickly you got here. Some aspects might seem stable and unchanged but that allows you to move others exponentially without the distractions of other aspects of life getting in the way. Find peace in your accomplishments and be gentle with yourself on the ones that are still working themselves out.

Don't let circumstances determine your day. Choose to be calm and go with the flow. You can't control everything, especially when it involves working with others. Be yourself and speak the truth. There is no judgment except you towards yourself. Notice when you are doing that and stop. You won't get better until you shift how you are viewing it. If you are wallowing in the pity party mentality, then you are keeping yourself in a low vibration where it can strive. You need to shift it to a higher vibration where it can heal. Do you want to heal or have others feel bad for you? Choose how you want to address it mentally and physically. You are getting better even if it's not by much. Take time to prioritize your health and handle it.

IT'S NOT A CHORE. IT'S EVOLUTION

Life is not a countdown. It's good to have events to change the routine and to look forward to but don't ever look back at how you let time pass waiting for the next big thing instead of enjoying the present. There is more here to do than milestone events and interactions. There are key choice points and realizations that lead you to new places physically or spiritually. Just keep going and use the days between milestones to make a difference in your overall journey or direction. They are only filler days if you use them as such, otherwise they are building blocks and part of something bigger. You are already on your way to building a new future. Do you want to add more blocks or watch tv? There are times to relax and times to grow. Which one feels better to you? Use your time wisely. You never know how much you have left.

———

Be present in your day. See what has shifted or still needs to be grounded within you after the holidays. Every experience has an effect. Find what has found peace or is still out of sorts trying to adjust back to your routine life. Not all changes are bad but see how they affect you mentally and physically. Are they bringing you peace or worry? What parts of you are still mentally struggling to come back to balance? Pull yourself out of the thought patterns surrounding trying to understand how others choose to live in a place you couldn't wait to leave. Bring yourself back to the present and where you are now. Bring your thoughts back to your life and your accomplishments. You owe no one explanations for the life you live or how you choose to view things.

Let it all go. You aren't physically there anymore. Let the complaints and grievances stay there and focus on your gratitude in the here and now. Don't keep pulling yourself back into uncomfortable situations mentally. Accept that your views and values are different due to your life experiences. There is no right or wrong. You have adapted and accepted. Come back into your current life. See how it feels after the mental gymnastics you have been through. See how it feels to have chosen to live somewhere with a warmer climate, with more diversity, in a younger generation willing to change what doesn't fit instead of tolerating and complaining for years. Notice the differences but bring yourself back to the peace of the life you are living. You are back home now. You are safe.

Connect to where you are in the present, in this plane of existence. You are not separate. Separation is an illusion. Everything is interconnected and part of the whole. You just need to remember and focus on that connection to be in balance with what is around you in the moment. Remind yourself that you are not alone. Your presence and connection are felt on many levels by different species and realms. You are making a difference on so many levels by just being you, by exploring the unknown, by learning, by growing, sharing, and connecting to those around you. Share your presence and who you really are. You don't need to force beliefs on others for them to connect and see something in themselves due to their interaction with you. Healing often happens on levels you can't always see but it's a catalyst to promote the changes needed.

Just be present. Come back to the present when the to-do lists, worries, and anxiety start to feel real. Remind yourself it's your perspective or fears that produce the negative reactions or stress you are feeling. In the present nothing is really happening but you just being, just breathing. The rest is not happening, in the now. Bring yourself back as often as you need. Connections are always there. You just need to bring your awareness to them. Come to your place of peace, to your place of knowledge, that there is more, and you are more. You are not alone. You are never alone. Remember who you really are, an infinite spark of the whole.

CONTROL AND THE FLOW

You need to focus. You are going through the motions again. Where is your awareness? You need to be present to gain the most from life, but you are mentally onto the next task while you are in the middle of something else. Life is not a series of tasks to be done. I know it feels that way, but that's how you are choosing to view it. You should not be "scheduling in some fun" you need to live life in such a way that's it not a calendar event and constant obligations.

It's all just a matter of shifting how you see things, how you experience things, and what you want out of life. If you see everything as an item to be checked off, then it will feel like work. If you view it as an experience, you can be present for and gain something from, then you can start to enjoy life again. How are you viewing things? How do you want to experience your day?

Obligations are a part of life. That doesn't mean you have to push through and start living after they are over. You spend so much of your time not being present and disassociating yourself from what you are doing when it's not something you enjoy. Find a way to enjoy it by adding music or lectures to that time. Make a game of your chores. Find peace in folding clothes or washing dishes. Listen to the sounds. Feel the textures. Find a way to be in the moment and enjoy it. You can't live life in a state of annoyance over the nuances. They will always be there. How will you react to them? That's where you have control.

Breathe when you feel it building when frustrations start to surface. Breathe. It brings you back to your body to the present, where you can remind yourself it's temporary. This too shall pass. Take back the control you are giving that item or event. It's crazy how much of your power you give to an email, or an inconvenience. Your need to control and not go with the flow has you viewing life as a road littered with speed bumps when you want to just cruise, but you are adding those bumps. You are the one refusing to go with the flow, causing you to need to slow down and push through. You are stopping yourself and acknowledging the wrong things. Stop fixating on where you have no control. That's not going to change things or force others to fix or adjust or do the things how you feel they should. It's just going to frustrate you, drain your energy, and leave you unwilling to do anything at the end of the day.

Don't you see that you are giving your power away, that you are fighting the flow of things, that you are not trusting what you receive as you want to control and "schedule your day to fit within the box you feel it should fit in? Until you learn to trust or let go, it will continue to feel like a struggle. You get to make that decision. Do you want peace, or do you want things your way? It's up to you. Change what you can but accept and let go of that which you can't.

It's a new day so live it. Gather your energy and start something, go somewhere, do something. Every day you can have a new lease on life. It can be a new beginning, a start. You don't have to wait for a special occasion or start of a month to start over. Progress can happen whenever you choose. It doesn't need a calendar boundary. What do you want to accomplish? Where is your destination? The sooner you start the sooner change can happen.

Promises of a calendar date are an excuse. If you have an excuse before you can start how likely will you have an excuse to stop? You need to pay attention to your habits and what they are really saying about your dedication or desire for the future. You need to build a firm foundation which can't be done with excuses. Where did they come from? How do they serve you? Are they preventing you from progressing?

Be aware of what is really happening at the start of your day. Are you starting with dread and a to do list, or excitement and wonder? If you are set up to begin the wrong way, it sets the tone for your entire day. Are you looking for excitement or a chore? Are you waiting for it to be over before it even begins? Look at how you spend your time. If it seems like a chore, add something into your day to look forward to. Add music or a podcast, a treat for finishing a task, meet up with friends in the evening. You create your day. What are you infusing into it?

Accountability is key. If you aren't aware of your defaults, then they are running the show, not you. Ask questions when you aren't at your best or when you are feeling annoyed. Find where the issues are and address them. The sooner you take accountability the sooner you are back on course and living a life that brings you joy. Too often we just get used to, "this is just how things are" but never ask why or what you can do to change that. Life is malleable and can be shaped to what you want it to be. It might take some work, but wouldn't you rather wake up excited, rather than counting down until you can go back to bed?

Compare how you feel now to how you felt in your 20's. You did not have the resources or knowledge you have now, yet you lived your days to the fullest, going out most nights, plans all weekend long. When did that stop? Why did that stop? As much as you might have grown out of some of that, what did you replace it with that was comparable to make you excited about each day? Growing up does not mean giving up on happiness or joy. Some people find it by raising children and living through their experiences, some by what they create, some with travel, classes, making new friends. What are you incorporating into your life to enhance your enjoyment of life? Find what brings you joy, do more of that. Wake up excited again. This is the life you are creating. Live it.

There's a difference between going after something and being impatient about your expectations on how it unfolds. You should pursue your goals and be driven. That's the conviction behind the changes needed to see results, but impatience is part of controlling when **you** feel those results should show themselves and how. It is not the same as being driven. You can be driven and still understand that things happen in their own time. You can still be driven and not forcefully control every single detail and expectation of outcome. Patience and impatience play a part in progress. Impatience can cause you to lose sight of the big picture or lose steam and give up. Patience is an understanding that there are always things beyond your control when you are doing something new, and it allows you to be open to how that can benefit the outcome and timing of results.

You worry too much about how you want to see your future unfold and your impatience causes discouragement. It's not that things aren't still unfolding. It just a slow bloom and waiting for you to polish up a few areas before it comes into view and envelopes you into its essence. Step back from your expectations and see the bigger picture. Figure out the missing steps between when you started and what result you want. Sometimes you are the hold-up, because physically you might be ready but mentally you don't even believe in yourself.

Be driven to sort out the smaller details. Your journey is not just going from point A to point B. There is a whole journey between those destinations that needs to happen and needs your attention as well. In order to not fail you need to focus on the journey and the present moment. Keep in mind where you are going, but what in the present do you need to put your focus on to make the future work effectively?

IT'S NOT A CHORE. IT'S EVOLUTION

What are you missing that you are perceiving as impatience could be the tweak or idea that is needed for success. Don't trip yourself up with negativity because life won't fit into the box you made for it. Life is to be organic and free flowing. That's how it breathes and brings energy into experiences. Let it breathe. Let it work its magic.

Be aware of the present and what steps are next. If you are running, you could trip or miss something. You need to adjust your pace and your view of progress. You aren't even giving yourself credit for how far you've come because you are so consumed by wanting to be there now. You lost sight of why you are even doing this or why now is not the time. You have several goals competing at any given time, and some need you to be where you are now to finish unfolding. If you skip the steps, you lose the opportunities life is trying to provide you. You aren't stuck, you are just focusing on the wrong things. Breathe and go with the flow. Be present. The future will come in its own time.

You can be in the moment and still moving toward something. It's being strapped to results and outcomes that is what you need to beware of. This doesn't mean you aren't to take accountability for your actions, or inactions. You still need to take steps to start a journey but be flexible on the destination and what that looks like. When you start setting expectations on what everything should look like you are setting yourself up for self- judgement. IE: This is where I should be now. This is what this should look like. I should have seen the results already. I'm not good enough compared to someone doing the same thing. When you start seeing these thoughts pop up it's from your need to control instead of surrendering.

Instead of being rigid on goals, make them vague and open to adjustments. Leave room for your personal growth to find better solutions, for the universe to get you there by different paths, for it to be part of the journey and not a destination or end result. Leave it open to be something more or bigger than what you could conceive when setting your course. It's ok for detours and life lessons. It's ok to realize this goal doesn't make sense after incorporating new information. But yes, still set up a direction to head out, and start taking steps. Just don't be so set on how many stops and which roads are the "correct" way to get there. Be open to what might work better as you go and as you learn. It might not be the correct results for where you need to be but if you are too focused you might miss the real journey and the actual destination.

Process is the learning and evolving end of making changes in your life. There is not a set way for that to look as it changes as you change. It could be steps and tasks you need to complete. It could be ideas and people you need to connect with. It still involves changes on some level, and it is getting you to someplace new. Process could be considered the journey. A journey often indicates a set destination and in order to make progress you need to focus on what you can work on and adjust and learn now, not how it is relevant for the set result you are seeking.

When you are seeking you are focused on a particular thing which means you miss everything you came in contact with, in that moment. The present could be giving you clues and resources but if you are seeking and not really being present you will miss everything you are being given to help you find what you need. Blinders are correct and you are the one that needs to realize what you are doing and make the changes to resolve the issues. You can't keep moving forward without awareness of what is happening around you. You need to be present, you need to observe, and you need to be aware. You miss so much when you aren't looking around and seeing what is going on. It is up to you to stop, turn your head, and actually see what is happening. You need all the information to make informed decisions. That can't happen until you remove the blinders, let go of results, and surrender to the process with an open heart. Let your heart lead not your mind. Feel where you are going.

———

Go back to the basics. When life starts moving you need to go along with it. It's easier to go with the flow than to stand still and get bombarded with the waves. Ride them to shore. Use them to your advantage. Make the most of things instead of looking for faults and issues. Finding faults is not a scavenger hunt. There are no prizes. It only brings more stress and more separation. It leads to more negativity and problems because that's where you choose to put your attention. What if you tried to find the positive instead? What if you tried to just be present instead of focusing on what you can't control? Maybe things are feeling chaotic for a reason and that reason is a benefit and you don't even see it.

Stop and take a breath. Take stock of what you are doing and what is really happening. How much value are you giving to things that don't really matter? How long are you holding on to unimportant things? Why are you grasping instead of releasing? You are in control of these things, yet you give it up and try to control the things you can't. It's a lost battle and doesn't even need to be a fight. You are stressing yourself out and creating your own problems.

Let it go. Let it all go and move along with things. Don't fight the current. Don't fight change. This is what you came here for. Learn to adjust, accept, and incorporate and make things better. This is all temporary and is leading somewhere. Keep following to find out where that is.

———

Going with the flow involves letting go of control. The next step is letting go of the anger and frustration created when things out of your control happen and the need to judge how they should have or could have been different. Part of control is feeling you know best and that things should go a certain way or that people or companies should treat others in a certain manner, but you aren't in charge of that. You don't have a say over other's actions and consequences created. You only have control over how you react.

Acceptance in the moment, in the public eye is fine, buy what are you doing later? You're analyzing, judging, being frustrated, angry and not letting go of what happened despite it being over. Be in the now not judging what now "could have been if not for..." Be in the now that you are actually in not mulling over your "I'd rather be..."

It's very difficult to let go when you are wrapped up in "how you would have" or "if they had only" or "what if I had never even". That time has passed. You are wasting the time you have now by staying in your judgement and anger and re-living it. You are looking for others to validate how betrayed you feel instead of accepting. Just because you didn't yell at a service provider at the time doesn't mean you accepted things. Acceptance means in the moment and moving forward. Circling back to judgement and complaining is not acceptance.

Do you want to keep feeling these negative feelings or do you want to move on and take back your life and the free time you were given? Actions speak louder than words. Now is your time for control. Control your emotions, your self-talk, and how you spend your time. Control what you allow for yourself after an event.

You are allowed to feel betrayed, or frustrated, but set a time for that feeling then release it. Don't make it your new talking point. Don't keep reliving an experience you didn't like. This is when you let it go. This is when you shift. This is when you put into practice what you already know and have grown from this instead of shifting back into old paradigms. Be the change you want to see. Your unhappy place is your mind and thoughts, not the world after the event.

Focus on what you gained and what you are going to do next. Use your time to evolve, not sulk. Make good out of what you viewed as bad. You are the one giving everything labels. Choose better ones more in line with where you are headed and what you want to feel. The rest doesn't matter. This too will all be a memory soon, so enjoy the time you have. Spend it focusing on what you want not judging what you don't want. Let it go. Breathe. Move on.

Being organized is fine. It helps keep order, helps find things, and keeps track of what hasn't been done, but you still need to have flexibility in how things get done and where things end up. Organization is starting the groundwork, providing space, giving value, importance, and structure to things. It's the set-up stage for the actions that need to be taken to see results. Those actions are where you have the switch from organized to controlling. Actions are something that can be controlled, can be done in different ways, add time or add effort to a situation. This is where you need to remain open. This is where you need to let down your guard and be open to new methods and new ideas on how you make it to the result. You can then organize the order of attack for what comes through but the actual path and methods, that's what you need to be open minded about.

You actually need the organization end or things would never get completed. You need to realize if there are extra steps, what order makes sense, or who or what resources you have. Those are all important parts of the process. It's the trusting aspect and open to new ideas and asking for help that you need to stop trying to control. The time frame and exactly how it should look or feel that needs to be released. You can visualize what you are looking to do but don't be disappointed when it arrives differently. It's releasing expectations. It's not limiting yourself and what you are capable of. Be open to a different more exciting version of your life. Be open to dreaming bigger.

———

Don't shut yourself off from opportunities due to how you want things. Be open to other solutions, or new ideas to get you to where you are going. Change can be subtle or an overhaul. Gather your research and make informed decisions. Be open to things being different than your limited expectations on how you wanted to see things unfold. Don't be so set in your ways or your need to control that you miss opportunities that could paint a more complete picture for you. Just because you can't figure out the overall doesn't mean these additional steps aren't part of it. Just don't close yourself off to different versions or scenarios.

You can only control so much, but the universe sees what it could be and can fill in the details. You need to be open to them, even if you don't understand them. That does not mean they are a wrong turn it just means we have greater things in store for you still. Don't close yourself off. See your potential. Figure out your gifts. Don't sell yourself short due to fear or where you are now. You are growing and expanding. That growth opens doors to new directions in life that you might not even realize yet. We have more in store for you than you realize but we need you to not hold yourself back. Be open. Be willing. Be motivated for change. Trust in something outside of yourself and see how far you can go.

———

Let things be. Let them happen as they do and work on acceptance. Not everything is a fight or battle. It's your need to control that causes the resistance, but if you just let things fall as they might, accept, and move on, then everything can be in flow and moving. You can't keep holding onto a rock in the current. You need to move with the water to avoid being battered. The speed will eventually slow but for now move with things. Realize what is your responsibility and what is not and act accordingly. You try to control things that aren't yours, but don't take ownership of what you should be owning up to. Where is your focus? Why are these your priorities? Where are you headed from here?

Find where adjustments can be made in your own life and how you spend your free time. That is where you have control. Use it accordingly. Are you reading just to pass the time or are you incorporating learning and concepts? You need to realize how you view things and their value in your life. Where do you want to go from here? What changes need to be made to get there? Are you stopping yourself from making those changes? If so, why, and how do we address that? Take back control of your future. Implement a strategy and timeline and start working toward it. Don't keep letting time pass. Use it to your advantage. You'd be surprised how far you can go when you are focused on a goal.

Surrender is not necessarily giving up, it's a release. It's like removing pressure before it causes an explosion. It always depends on the context. Some things are holding you back and once released, allow you to move forward. There is a positive that can come of surrendering if it's something that does not serve you. It allows you to move with the flow instead of fighting it. It shows you where your attachments and priorities are. A white flag is often peace over war. Everything is in context. Which side of the coin is it today?

Where can you release your need to control and surrender to how things are and where you should be? Stop the need to fight. Everything does not need to be a battle. It's your need to hold tight or push your will that causes the resistance that you are fighting. Why are you holding so tight? What are you afraid to lose? What are you preventing yourself from gaining?

There is progress in motion, in moving forward, in surrender. There are lessons and traction to be gained, a new direction ahead, a new chapter to write. Are you fighting a battle you created? Are you ready to release that need for control and let things be as they should and go with the flow? Release what is holding you back. Submit to the Universe and where it wants to lead you. Surrender to your new life and the benefits that it will bring you. Raise the white flag of peace in your life and breathe into the changes that are coming. It's nothing to fear, but something to celebrate.

—————————

When you complicate things, it adds extra layers of work and dread. Always assuming a new thing is going to be difficult is a mental deterrent to accomplishment. You psych yourself out before you even begin and view simple things as having possibly been done wrong. You are waiting for the other shoe to drop. It's your view and negative outlook that often complicates things and makes them seem worse than they really are.

There is simplicity in the universe, a natural flow. You would not be given something what is beyond your capabilities. Most things can be broken down into simpler tasks that then built into the mountainous task you were given. You need to step away from the whole and look at the components and build one brick at a time instead of overwhelming yourself at the sight of the overall picture. You can simplify whatever you need to for comprehension purposes. Most things start small and build as their normal development so start there. Build up until completion.

IT'S NOT A CHORE. IT'S EVOLUTION

Clarity comes with understanding and dissecting things. It's how learning works. You need to understand the concepts and how things came to be to appreciate what they are now. All things start small, from trees, humans, ideas, and companies. It's a place to start, to learn, to grow, and to evolve. Start simple and grow. Pretty soon what seems complicated is not and your comprehension of it becomes bigger than the original task. Break things down then build them up. Nothing is too big for you to accomplish if you look at the pieces first then start building your puzzle.

Remove the resistance you have created and let things flow naturally. Don't block your own stream for fear of what's happening up stream. Trust that whatever is flowing to you is appropriate and necessary for your journey and surrender your need to control. You can't control the air, just breathe. You can't control the water, just drink. There needs to be some trust that not everything is on your plate, your responsibility, or will fall apart if you don't put yourself into the mix.

Notice what things you are trying to steer that are on autopilot and let be. They were set up that way for a reason. Learn to trust even if you think you know a better way, and definitely if it's something you don't understand. Trust should not have so many perimeters and hoops to jump through. There is a difference between being accountable for your life and trying to control all aspects of it. Find the boundaries. Find what you are trying to control that maybe needs you to let go or walk away from. If you are having to put too much effort into changing something, then maybe it's you or the direction that needs to change instead. See where your time and energy are going. Question what happens if you release the need to control how it will flow. If it carries you downstream to something else anyway, then those boulders to direct the water weren't necessary.

Take the stress and obligation off your plate. Not everything is for you to control. Let flow and let be. Trust the stream is leading you where you need to go. Don't try to force staying at a bank that was just a rest stop. Keep going to great destinations, larger openings, better opportunities. Let the river take you home.

WORKING WITH OTHERS

You are a warrior. You must be strong, not necessarily physically but mentally. Find that strength within you and flex those muscles. There is work to be done and you need to be a leader in this revolution. You need to hold the flag and remind others why this is important. We aren't asking you to fight as much as we are asking you to inspire and guide.

Be the leader. Hold the map. Give Directions. Troubleshoot Issues. You are more capable than you think. You are already starting to put people on their path. Give them that nudge they need. Leadership does not mean yelling in front of a group of eager troops, sometimes its side conversations, building someone's confidence in themselves, and empowering them to be their own guide. It's subtle but effective at getting the job done, but not needing glory.

Needing occasional reassurance is one thing, needing to constantly feel you are in charge is another. You need to learn the difference between trusting your instinct and needing to be in control. You can't help others if you don't work on your own shortcomings. You lead by example. Even if it's just one person at a time, the change will be felt. You just need to remember who you are, why you are here, and how powerful you are when you are in the flow of things.

Start over as many times as you need. As long as you keep moving, we are making progress. Realize how you feel in the present moment when you do things. If they make you feel love find ways to incorporate them more. If they make you feel miserable, how do you shift that to a more positive experience? You are not stuck. Your perspective is stuck. It's defaulting to view things a certain way and you need to shift your view or shift the things. You can't stay in a negative vibration willingly. You need to transmute it and move on with your day. Things aren't as bad as you make them out to be. Some of it is you wanting to control a situation and not being able to and getting combative as a result. Learn to choose your battles. Do you want peace, or do you want things to be done how you "feel" they should be? If you can't control how others handle their responsibilities then you need to accept and move on, not fixate, and frustrate.

You are going to feel really silly when you look back at how much time you spent being angry over something that really doesn't matter, because you just couldn't let it go. Maybe it keeps coming up so you can work on it, yet you keep reacting in the same way expecting different results. Check your feelings in the moment, they will let you know. If you feel you need to apologize with how you responded to something maybe that's an indication that you could have decided on a different approach or tactic. Make the shift and find the solution. Maybe it's just where you are prioritizing things that is the problem. At the end of the day, you need to learn to let things go. These are not important struggles. They are wasting your time and energy.

No running. No Hiding. This is it. This is what you came here for. You can't shy away from progress once it gets difficult. You have to grow and expand with it. You can't hide from your potential. This is who you were meant to be, embrace it, hold it, make it your own. Wear it like a favorite sweater. It's yours now. Come into your potential. Be that better version of yourself. You don't need to shy away from who you really are for fear of acceptance. As long as you love and accept yourself the right people will gravitate to you and support who you really are and what you are capable of.

IT'S NOT A CHORE. IT'S EVOLUTION

It's ok to lose some people along the way. That's just how personal growth happens. You can't have different yet surround yourself with the same. As you grow, some will grow with you, others will try to hold you back or keep you small. Pay attention to who you surround yourself with and that their intent does not become yours. Some are not comfortable with change, either their own or those around them, and will try to keep things as they are. Don't let others fear prevent you from greatness. Don't let others doubt become your own doubt. Remove the tethers to the life you are living if they are holding you back. Bring with you the ones that are curious and want to follow. You cannot feel guilty about ending unhealthy one-sided relationships. It doesn't not mean you are an unloving human. It means you value yourself and your worth and are setting healthy boundaries. There is no shame in that. It's the only way growth can happen. They might have served you for earlier parts of your life, but sometimes you need to step out on your own and find out what you are capable of.

Come into the light with what you've learned, who you really are, and where you want to be. Be honest with yourself and not ashamed. If you aren't confident in your journey others will sense that. It's hard to support a leader who seems lost, but if you are open and honest about where you are, where you are headed, and that it might still be a way to go, there will be respect for that progress, curiosity about the changes, and support to help get you there. You don't need to have all the answers, but you do need to buy into what you are selling, or it will just feel like a child paying pretend. You need to own it, to live it. Others would have no choice but to believe it also.

You have taken the steps, now you must own up to your progress. Look how far you have come. See how much difference has already started to unfold. See it for yourself and be proud. Step into who you are becoming. Try it on. Adjust till it fits. The future looks good on you.

Everything is not a war. There doesn't always have to be a battle to make change. Violence and anger do not produce the type of change that is lasting. Intimidating and forcing others to live a lifestyle they don't want is not going to make for a peaceful outcome. There is a lack of logic there and a constant cycle of resentment for that which was lost. There is a logic behind failure sometimes, but often when someone is determined and their objective is one-sided, that logic is lost or becomes irrelevant. They will destroy themselves or an entire country rather than admit to being wrong.

There are certain personality types that are too lost to ego to try to reason with. They have given up too much control and the malleable human who could learn and expand is no longer in charge. They see only this plane, the here and now, and want a legacy with no concept of consequences. You can't reason with someone who is too far gone and determined to destroy. They can only be taken down by those closest with quickest resolve, but that rarely happens.

There are constant wars due to set and rigid thinking. Longing to keep things a certain way to fit into a certain box for a value system that did not grow with the times and is obsolete now. When you put too much emphasis on the physical world you lose possibilities of something more or something better. Families are passing down their destructive belief patterns and it becomes another generation's burden. You brainwash them with these values at an age when they are impressionable and surround them with the same until they don't believe or know the truth once it is shown to them.

They can't see something that does not exist in their realm of experience or will not be believed by those they surround themselves with. It's easier to just defend false beliefs than to have your world and values shattered by evolving or changing with new information. They want to defend what they started building rather than scrap it and start over since they already lost so much time to it. You can't remove blinders that are permanently glued on and grown over. It's too much a part of them.

It's a whole other subset of society. Location is the determinant of the type of freedom you will have to explore new ideas and where you can live your life. If you are born into war and a set culture, you won't be given as many opportunities as in a place of peace and open-mindedness. It does not make all people from a location bad, but it becomes hard to break a cycle that is part of the culture. There's a tit for tat and punishment for not following the values that were passed down. You need to flee or continue the endless fighting.

Someday this will end, and you can look back and objectively see how stupid it all was, but in the moment, for those people, this is all they know. This is how they are raised. They aren't given a choice for something better. The system needs to be shattered as they are all prisoners. Education is part of it, but so are resources. You can't grow change without providing the seeds for it.

____

What are we creating that is new if everything has already been done and is just repeating the past? Different versions of the same things, small tweaks, minor changes but still the same. Is it different mindsets viewing it that makes it seem new? New is in the eyes of the beholder and the expansion of their limited view. The removing of blinders to finally see what's always been there, but in a different time or context that makes sense for them now.

Vision is different for everyone, as is perception. The viewer decides what they make of life and that's what makes it different for everyone. You can't dictate or regulate how someone filters what they know or what they've seen. It has all their own perspective thrown into the mix directing them to use what is experienced in the context of where they are on their evolutionary path. What you see as a child looks different than the same thing as an adult, as you have a different mindset and knowledge to associate, different intent as to what to look for and receive from the experience. It's never the same for everyone. You'll even associate with different characters later in life watching the same movie. Who are you now? Who were you then? Who are you going to be in the future?

You must continue to create as you never really know who your audience will be or what they will receive from what you share. It could be nothing or it could be the missing piece of the puzzle they have been struggling to complete. You are able to reach so many with such little effort. Let them decide the value. Don't withhold for fear that it has no worth. Worth and value are on an individual level. You just hold up your own and let them decide for themselves.

You can't make decisions for others or determine what is best. You don't know the whole story, their journey, truths, struggles, or what they came here to learn. Though it's nice to want to help, you can only offer. The other person needs to make the decision to accept and to incorporate it into their lives otherwise it serves no purpose. It's like buying someone clothes you think they'd like. If it's not their style, you have wasted money and it'll never be worn. You cannot force others to see things the same as you. You can share and give context, but their ability to see and understand is still up to them.

Agitation of someone not seeing the truth is a large frustration. It's hard to understand why they can't comprehend basic concepts, things that make sense and can be proven. This has always been a part of the human condition. You have different levels of comprehension, education, and knowledge. Sometimes this can lead to the subjugation of large parts of society. Some people would rather remain in the dark and let decisions be made for them rather than risk the backlash of having a voice and it not being received well by the masses. It's a matter of how convicted are you in what you want to see in life? How much do you care? How much change do you want to have a hand in?

If you aren't making the changes then when they go wrong, you can't be held to blame, but that is not really living. Unfortunately, that's all the more power some people seek or see for themselves. You can force their eyes open, but you still can't make them see. How blind are you to what happens in your life?

———

You need to have a basic understanding to know where someone is coming from. The more you learn the better equipped you are to relate on different levels to help those that might need your service. There is no lost time in learning. Its value is immeasurable. Your proficiency is only needed if you plan to teach something to others, but general knowledge of concepts can go a long way. How do you want to help others? How can you be of service? You are a light shining so others can see. They are drawn to you like moths to a flame. They don't always know why but there is something in them that sees that light that makes you familiar, that offers them something they need on their path. It is your job to decipher what is missing. Open that door and let them connect to their own inner light so they may shine as well.

You get to be the lighthouse guiding people home safely, back to who they are, who they were always meant to be. You are a reminder that they are safe, that the turbulence and darkness were just lessons, part of their journey. All they need to do is follow the light, reconnect to who they are, and they are home again. Be that beacon of hope for them, that reminder, that catalyst. Bring them out of the darkness. Bring them home.

You can't take on other people's problems, but you can try to understand where they are coming from, so they don't feel so alone. Often when you are caught up in stress and figuring out hardships you go within. You then forget that you could always ask for help and don't have to go at it alone. Sometimes they just need to talk to sort it out or hear it out loud to understand it themselves. An ear is often better than unsolicited advice, but use your judgement. Listen and only give if asked. It's their life to conquer. Sometimes you are a shoulder, sometimes the other perspective they need to see things from. Being available is the important part though so they know they have support, whatever that may need to be for them.

Show compassion no matter the story or your perspective. Though often people create their own suffering for different reasons, all you can do is show you care, for them to know they will make it through. You don't need to relate to show compassion. You just need to be present and support them. Don't take on their stress. Let it be theirs to solve. It's their journey. They need to take the steps. You can guide but the steps are still theirs. Provide the map, the compass, or the snacks, but stay your course. You can empathize without taking on the burden. Learn to do that. See the problems from outside yourself and release once they are back on their way. Set them free so the universe doesn't hold them back due to your attachment.

Empathy is not a superpower. Being able to tell someone is in pain or going through something allows an opportunity for healing. However, it is not your responsibility to take on their problems or alleviate things for them. That is still their life to sort out. You can offer an ear, perspective, or a session but do not take on their problems as your own. Your personal development allows you to see solutions and opportunities they aren't aware of, which is frustrating to you. You know it's resolvable if they take accountability and open themselves up for change, but that is still their life and their steps to take. You can only open the door. You can't push them through it. If they aren't ready, they will just stand at the threshold of change. However, when they are ready, the pace they enter and how far they go will amaze you, but it must be their time and their choice. It's their lessons to learn, their opportunities to be had, the universe's alignment for them.

You can bring them to the door, to awareness, but it's ultimately their choice to take those next steps. Find the balance between helping and trying to run someone's life for them. Which are you trying to do and who's getting the benefit? Let them know you have concerns. Let them know there are alternative ways to live. Then put it back in their hands to make the next move. You don't know their journey or what they are going through. Focus on your journey. They will catch up when it is their time and will bridge the gap, but it's got to be their choice, not yours.

Keeping the peace often involves deciding where your priorities lie. How important is making your point? If it's falling on deaf ears or someone who is not on the same level of understanding and is more interested in being right than listening or having a two-way discussion, then it's not a battle worth fighting. They are shut off from anything other than their desire to be heard and dominant. So, you need to decide if you should just choose peace and take back your time. You can't convince or force someone to be reasonable or listen to thoughts or ideas outside of their set beliefs and are just wasting time and energy. Your knowledge of their character trait plays a bigger part than the discussion. It's not validating them. It's knowing when goals are not aligned. Taking to a brick wall is not good use of anyone's time.

Sometimes the request or action takes less time than the refusal and conversations. Pick your battles. Choose peace and let things go. Don't spend the rest of your day annoyed over something that took 10 minutes. Where are you giving up control? Are you letting inconveniences ruin your day or are you in charge? You can't change the past so why dwell on it. Learn what you need and move on. You have a future to build and need to move forward. When are you battling and when are you choosing peace? How important is pushing your will on others as opposed to enjoying your day and preserving your relationships? Where are your priorities? Choose peace.

Be in the moment. You don't need to adhere to anyone else's experience, comments, or judgment. Participate. This is your experience as well. Handle your obligations then decide what's best for you. It's your last day of downtime before tomorrow starts and you are busy. Keep yourself in the flow. Come back to a place of calm when needed. Take note of what still makes you feel anxious and why. This is a great opportunity to see what still needs addressed and adjusted. It does not mean there is something wrong with you. You all have different reactions due to the conditioning that you are still working through.

Determination and comfort level play a part for others. That does not mean you are falling behind. They have different obligations, finances, and expectations than you. You can't look at a stay-at-home mom's free time as a comparison of how much you are able to be involved or participate. You can't look at someone older with a spouse's income who didn't have high college prices and debt as a comparison of what you can financially participate in. Everyone has their own thing happening. There is no comparison or a need to compare. Everyone is at their own pace, on their own path, and they don't always run parallel even if the destination or one of the stops are the same. Remember this is just a stop, a way to learn a new skill. It's not your end goal. It's a connection and a building block on your path. You need to always be aware and surrender to the flow when it leads you in a new, better direction. Is this a pause or a stop? Rest and reflect. You are here to learn.

———

Generosity can be made of your time as well as tangible objects. Sometimes all someone needs is time and a safe space to be heard. Giving without anticipation of receiving comes from a place of abundance. When helping another is more important than what you physically receive or lose as a result, that's where love comes into play. The connection and support take center stage as you are growing along with them. Don't feel obligated though. Set boundaries and observe when it's appropriate to offer and when someone is being greedy and taking advantage of you. Not everyone comes from a pure place of intention. Be open but take care of yourself in the process. Don't judge yourself in the process for decisions you make. Just notice how you feel when you feel open and when you constrict. Find out why you feel one way or the other and explore.

Don't view giving as a chore. The holidays do create a scenario where you are put in a position where spending money equates to love, but that's not true. That's not how it works. Be honest about your financial constraints. It's not that you are less generous or care less. You need to be aware of what makes sense for you. If buying gifts makes you feel regret due to finances, then have those conversations. Everyone you buy gifts for understands. Be open and be honest. Holiday are not obligations. They are to be a chance for connection and reflection, not put into a box and putting yourself out. Work with your circumstances.

Adjust where you need to. Love is about acceptance and understanding. Give it a chance.

Find your voice but know when to use it. There are times where it is appropriate and times where the other is too closed off that anything outside of their belief system will cause tension and hostility. Know your audience. It does not mean you are silencing yourself. You are actually rescuing your time and energy, which is more important, especially when your voice won't be heard by the other due to their boundaries.

Holidays are different for everyone due to family structures, distances, and grievances. There is no picture perfect or ideal box to try to fold into. You receive what is appropriate for the combination of personalities and circumstances. As an adult you get to choose the amount of participation and the importance you place on the interactions you have. Carve out a piece and make it your own., You are aware by now what you are walking into. Choose the perspective you want to have of the situation you are in. Don't judge your experience by how you feel when others are enjoying their holiday. You aren't being let down or missing out. That's your expectation and ego. Focus on the connections. View it as a normal day, a random family visit, because it is just another day, another visit. Be present in your conversations. Be open to what is being shared. Notice the appreciation of the interaction. This is what you should view as thankful for. Find strength and peace in whatever you do. You are sharing a part of you when you share your time. Be that light on a gloomy situation.

You can bring yourself into tranquility whenever you need. It is your natural state when you are experiencing love. Remind yourself that the external stimulants are just that, external. You are observing what is happening but not being dragged downstream by it. Sit calmly at the shores without judgement but with curiosity and acceptance. Everyone has different responses due to who they surround themselves with, their external stimuli, their beliefs, and their priorities. It's not going to match yours and it doesn't have to be for them to experience or learn what they came here for. You can read a story without agreeing with a character's choices. It's just part of the plot, of the bigger story, the overall that's happening. They help the story get to where it is headed. Right or wrong are judgements not acceptance, and when you don't know the end of the book, you can't foresee why the character is doing what they are, but it plays out how it should in the end.

Don't let it get to you. You knew there was more, and you flew away from the nest to go see it. They accepted where they were and what they were told and never learned to fly. They believed the wings were decorative. With an open mind and experience you will understand how things come together but you can't look down on those who haven't had those experiences. Even if it was and still is their choice, because at the end of the day it is their life. Not everyone is here to figure it out. Some are just here for a smaller supporting role, to learn or experience things you might already have learned. Be patient and accepting. Bring yourself back to a place of peace as needed and remind yourself this is a visit not your normal life that you live. Be thankful for how far you have come from being on the edge of that nest wondering what would happen.

Let go of your judgement. You have more experience and openness to understanding. You can't wish that on others or have them understand what you see, know, or comprehend. It's hard to accept decisions or understanding that are opposite of yours and hear the complaints on changeable situations that others choose not to change, but it is their life. There is a reason you left. There is a reason it's only visits and not staying. It's their personal choice. You need to let them have what they believe is right for them with acceptance even if it's not what you'd choose, even if what they consider facts are not truth, even if there is a better way and you've already walked that path to your better life. These are their choices, their lives, their patterns, their defaults, and their limited boundaries. It's hard acceptance but that's all you can do. You saw different and be thankful you choose growth over following in that pattern. However you need to accept their lifestyle as much as they accept yours though they don't understand it. You don't need to agree or understand to accept and let go.

You've lost time and energy rolling the lack of logic of their lifestyle choices or their limited thinking around in your head trying to understand it. Sometimes it's not for understanding. When it's a brick wall the structure is strong and the amount of effort to remove brick by brick is not worth it. Let it stand where it stands. That's their foundation even if it's on sinking soil. You can only be accountable for you. Release the need to understand what does not suit you, and move on to living the life you built far away from those values and parameters. Be thankful that it is not your life and that you saw further than that box they stayed in. It is not your place to try to change them or add a view they are not interested in sharing or incorporating. They won't hit opposition in the life they built as they have surrounded themselves with those that share the same values, influences, and understanding. They don't see it as a problem in their circle as they are in that circle. It's like religious persecution, different ways of thinking being punished for not changing to what someone else views as correct or right. Acceptance and walking away is not hurting anyone. Let them have their opinions and you go back to the life you built that makes sense to you.

IT'S NOT A CHORE. IT'S EVOLUTION

Evolution is like that. As you learn and understand more, relating to those who stayed where they were becomes more difficult. This is why you find a new tribe who is at your level of evolution, so you can have those conversations and ability to relate, so you have that company, and don't get pulled back down or feel you are going crazy due to trying to relate to someone not on the same level. Part of changing is realizing not everyone joined you on that journey. Some stayed behind. You can meet them where they are, but you can't force them to understand what has taken you years to evolve into.

They are not stressing about the interaction. You didn't try to force your view or even share it with them. You observed only when there. Don't let it be one sided stress that you are inflicting upon yourself. Let it go. Accept where they are even if it's not your thing. Go back to your life. View it from outside of yourself. Don't get caught up in it. You left for a reason. Leave that negativity in that town, don't bring it back with you. You escaped. They choose to stay. Leave it at that.

You are forgiving their ego self in recognition of who they actually are and the connectedness you share. Any wrongdoing is a perspective you have toward a lesson they are learning on their journey and not a true reflection of who they are at the core and how they really feel if those obstacles on this plane were removed from their subconscious mind. It's hard to hold something against someone what is not a true reflection of them.

This does not mean you condone what has been done or the consequences of those actions whose lessons you might still be working through. You can acknowledge and have the recognition that those actions are of the ego and do not serve your journey and how you deserve to be treated. It's not the action you are forgiving. It's the soul in the human body who is working through something that you are forgiving. You are forgiving how their lessons might not be ideal for you, but you understand it might be part of their journey.

Condoning actions and forgiveness are not the same. You do not have to do both. See past the action. Step outside of what has occurred. You don't have to go back to being close to that person to forgive. You can forgive but still understand that they are still in this stage of learning which does not suit where you are and give distance or release their value from your immediate group. Learn. Don't keep putting yourself in harm's way. Sometimes forgiveness looks like setting that person free so that they can't do anymore harm and you have time to view them differently than their actions. That's ok too, but don't hold onto the bitterness and hate. That is not who you are and that is not the connection you truly have with them. Connect to love and release your view of the ego. Let it go. Free yourself.

There is always something to give. It doesn't always have to be money. There are ways you can support and help others with what you have. Sometimes all they are asking for is your time and someone to listen. It may not seem much to you, but you don't know what other support they have. Be available to help however you can. Be abundant. Be generous. Anything you give that is from your heart will come back to you multiplied.

This holiday season is to be about love. Bring that to the table during these visits. Focus on the good and not what is still in process. Things aren't necessarily bad, just not for you at this time, or pushing you to put your focus elsewhere. It's about how you want to view things that labels them as good or bad. Make these visits about the connections not about the inconveniences of weather or anything else that you are pushing through to bring them into reality. View yourself as a warrior making it through a battle fighting for something you believe in. It's ok to view snowy roads that way. You will conquer them and make it safe.

The meaning of a holiday is whatever you make it. There was always a time when this day meant nothing, meant something different, or was something more. Different cultures, religions, households, treat a holiday or this day, differently. There is no way to really find the root of how something once was when it's been something different in different aspects around the world. So, it does not make sense to have set expectations of how it should or shouldn't be celebrated or what that looks like as it's going to vary on so many levels.

The goal of the day is whatever you want it to be which could be coming together with those you love and spending time. Everything is what you make it and what you allow. Your mood, perspective, struggles, and expectations paint a picture. You can always pick up the brush and change it whenever you need to. Like any other day it's what you make of it and what you are willing to put into it that determines the outcome. Choose wisely. You never know what changes are going to happen in the coming year with divorces, deaths, moves, births, etc. The dynamics are never going to be the same. This is how this year's holiday is set up so be present in it and put irritations and politics aside and find common ground. Connect with others. Come from a place of love and acceptance. The rest is the ego, so tear up his invitation and choose love. Bring yourself into the mix and give the day your flavor. You're the exact ingredient needed to make this holiday complete.

What has changed? What has grown in your experiences, in your relationships? Did everything feel the same or can you notice the shifts in yourself, in others, or in your perspective of situations and interactions? Every interaction is a learning experience about yourself and how you view the world. Are your expectations directing you or are you open to what is actually happening?

The holidays shift you out of your normal day to day and into interactions and dynamics that aren't part of your constant. Are you viewing them with disdain because other's paths and views don't match yours? Are you open to understanding how their opinions are molded by their surroundings and experiences? There is learning in the dynamics of why they choose to live how they do and why you live how you live. One is not better than the other so don't view yourself superior for seeing what they choose to keep blinders on to. What they want or choose out of life does not need to match what you strive for in order for it to be appropriate for them.

If they don't know there is more, then finding joy where they are seems appropriate. You're seeing more and being willing to make changes to see and understand things, makes you who you are. Personal growth and evolution are a choice. It's a choice for others as well. Where they see a wall, you look for a door. Where they find comfort in enclosures you feel suffocated. Find value in your differences and how you want more and therefore see more. It's like a magic eye poster. You can't be upset that they don't see what you see looking at the same thing. Accept that this was their choice and keep going with your choices. You can always visit where they landed to see how far you have come.

INCORPORATING THE PAST

The past is a construction site. Hard hats, and just dust and scraps of what once was. Just a vague memory that ego changes over time until it's not even recognizable, until it's not even important, until it's been released and goes away. Floating away like a balloon in the breeze, blowing, bending, breaking branches down. Chopped, shredded, turning it into a lovely piece of furniture, a nick-nack, a trinket, a treasure trove for times gone.

Sit sipping, staring out the window of your soul. So much time has passed, but still so much time left ahead and things to be done, experiences to be had, feelings to share, differences to make. Make it up as you go, stumble, trudge, limp and dragging, crawling, but just still going. Trying to pull your life back together because you convinced yourself it's fallen apart, when really, it has not. You are just in a transition to something better. But change is scary, because you must trust in something inside you, that you put a muzzle on years ago, because you just wanted some peace and quiet. But now you can't hear the whisper, the whimper, the screams, the cries for help. You aren't sure if they are even there anymore. You know they are, but you lost your sense of hearing to the sounds of sanity, because you've been blasting noise, hammers, banging, noise. Concentration shot. Intuition shot.

End the drama and move forward with living. Things become easier when you love yourself. You stop caring about other's perspectives and continue to just be you without the drama or apologizes for being who you are. The fear of rejection is a perspective. When you can rise above letting others dictate how they want things and the bubble or comfort zone they have, acceptance and rejection disappear. This means the fear disappears and you have one less hurdle to jump over.

You are taught acceptance and rejection at a young age in school. Bad boy, good girl, pretty, smart, strong, all these adjectives putting people in competition with each other and telling them this is what is expected or accepted as right. You have the popular kids and the loners. This time frame is always something people get stuck on when looking back, because it's when you start to make that decision for yourself of, who am I, and do I want to continue to buy into this? This is why so many go away for college and become completely different people. They've removed the constraints of their family, their peers of 13 years, and can finally decide who they are. Those who stay and just accept the traditions aren't the most fulfilled and later in life break down as a result. There are patterns that happen as a direct result of acceptance of forced values during the formative years.

Partners and dating become difficult when you marry young because you don't know who you are or what your journey or mission is or that of the other person. You are assuming you are on the same path for growth. Your generation is at least breaking the chain and separating and getting divorced, so that the individual is free to make their own decisions.

We just need to remind you that even though you didn't stay in the box of marriage, kids, house, settling down, it doesn't mean you are missing out. It's quite the opposite. Those constraints can stifle a journey as you are more worried about your partner or kids, and you forget about yourself and your journey. Yes, some are here to be parents, to provide support for those on a bigger mission, but there is no shame in having a path that doesn't fit the mold. Things would never evolve if everyone stayed in the mold of what traditions and values were thrust upon them growing up. This is why you have the issues in small towns where they are closed-minded. They never expand their bubble, and their kids leave home and never come back. Look around you at those that left and those that stayed. See if there is a pattern, recognize who's still in the bubble and who got out.

Independence from what? The past is being celebrated in the present while disregarding what was fought for at the same time. Those that celebrate the hardest are those that understand the values the least. It's a very weird concept. Winners and losers, values, and families, all ripped apart. People are forced to try to believe something different than what was passed down to them. It's a pattern. Those that still believed England was their home, had to hide it. Then the civil war was similar where there were sides and a whole part of the country had to change how they believed things. However, in this war, they held onto the bitterness and the hate and hostility instead.

Evolution is difficult, as is change for a lot of people who are stuck in their ways and view how things benefit themselves and not others or the majority. These types of wars that force change are brutal but sometimes the only way changes were able to happen because the stalemate leaves transitions stuck otherwise. You can never convince everyone of anything even with all the facts. This is why some move to violence, to pushing their values, and quieting those on the other side of what they are pushing.

It's the history of the planet. It wasn't always that way but it's how things have been resolved on a large scale for years. Forcing values then subjugating the population after violence, and then celebrating that fight and the deaths of so many. They teach you similar in school with sports and everything being a competition. They threw away community and helping those less fortunate and acceptance. Even the small towns that have a close-knit community are closed off. Anyone new that enters is not accepted and needs to fall in line, because the community does not allow for and is suspicious of change. It's then closed off, secluded, and passing down values that are limited. Not understanding the outside world or other's plights, if it's not something they have experienced, is seclusion not inclusion.

There are just so many different ways people connect yet disconnect from each other at the same time. Different ways people choose to live, the values they feel are important, the small struggles and the bigger pictures. There's not a perfect place to live, so you choose according to your values and what you can and can't tolerate. That's why there are country people and city folks. Everyone has different ideas of what works, but it's all happening in one country that is supposed to be united.

It's like this in most places though. Different paces of living, different criteria for feeling safe, different prices of living. This is why everyone's experience is different and why everyone has their own point of view to offer and to teach others, to see how something else is or can be. The point is to remain open. Find the similarities, appreciate the differences, incorporate what makes sense. It should not be us vs them. Gain what you want from those wars, but just know that there were never good and bad guys, just different ways of living.

———

Why are you holding on? That's the question you need to ask. What are you hoping to gain from revisiting the past or getting frustrated about the future? If you can understand what part of you keeps bringing it up, you'll be better equipped to release it. Are you frustrated because you want to control the situation, feel anxious that you are forgotten, feel disrespected because your time is not being taken into consideration? That comes from being hurt in the past by an expectation of a negative outcome that wasn't resolved and is on edge as a result. You put money toward something that doesn't seem to be a priority to the people who took your money. You can either voice that to them on how that reflects on their services, or you release it to the universe and let it happen when it happens. To continue to be frustrated when you think about something you were excited about isn't necessarily productive or positive.

For your past, you still want to control how others experienced it. You are searching for validation in wanting them to understand how their actions made you feel. For them to take accountability, to validate what you had to work around. That's not how it works. You learned your lessons from your perspective of the experience. They need to learn theirs. You can't control their view, their feelings, or how they interpret their actions. You can't control them ever seeing or understanding your point of view. You don't need them to "get it" to have peace. You don't need them to validate the responses you had, nor do you need them to know you did what you could.

Sometimes you just need to accept the outcomes no matter the picture or light someone else painted you in, no matter how false or incorrect it is. It's their painting too, their view. They are valid in what they experienced even if it never matches up to how you experienced the same event. You were ok with your reasons for leaving. You need to be ok with their actions at the time. That was their choice for who they were at that moment and the beliefs and values they had. Their lessons weren't the same as yours. You can only take what is yours when you go. They get to decide what they leave with and what they toss.

Think how much freer you would feel if when you think back, you didn't view things as right or wrong, good or bad, and just viewed them as, this is what I learned and I am grateful for that, and you release the rest. Meditate on it, ask if there is anything else you need to learn from the event and ask for the energy to be released back into the universe. Let it go. Look at it from outside not "in" the situation and turn off the show after it is over. Don't get pulled down into feeling guilt, anger, frustration, or any negative feeling for something that is done and ended. It's over, the benefits received, the lessons learned. So, let the feelings be released. Laugh at the person you were then and what you didn't know and how silly you were to stay. Find strength in that you left, learned, and moved on. And then do just that.... Move on.

———————————

Release your past. You still have events that are stuck. Forgive them and forgive yourself. Remember your age. Are you going to let a teenager dictate your life? You were just becoming aware of things, and you were highly influenced by what others thought about you, all while being guarded and on damage control at home. It was a bad combination that created situations that stuck, and need released. If you are going to go back mentally then feel into how it makes you feel now. Pull out the lessons you learned, then shift what happened. Find the good in the experience. Notice you don't remember all the details of the apology you got but the event you remember like it was yesterday. That's the part that needs to be released. Why is that event even still have power? It has no reason to still have power when time and the people who were there have all moved on.

Hold it in your hand. Release it to the Earth. Transmute the energy and let it go. It doesn't mean you forget the memory. It means you view it outside of yourself like a movie, not within getting distressed, replaying, or creating new scenarios. Think of the time lost in that mind game. Think how much online training you could have made it through during that same time. Where would your time better serve you? Let it go and move on. There are whole chunks of your life that never come up. Why are those 4 years of high school so important when you planned to move way at the end anyway? Release it all. You aren't that person anymore.

Calm yourself. You create disease when you aren't at peace. You have spent days mentally still frustrated and wondering why you are sick. You are holding on to negativity instead of releasing and coming back to the present. Start to release that stress and frustration and see if your cold doesn't leave with it. This is all temporary. Are you going to give into it or push past it? Are you convincing yourself that you are worse than you are, or do you need the rest? Enter a place of calm and see how you feel.

Free yourself from your past. You keep pulling yourself there and putting those shackles back on to yourself. You aren't there right now and when you are you know it's just temporary and a visit. There is nothing that can force you to go back to living there again. Everyone is grown, the circumstances are gone. Breathe a sigh of relief that you made it through and release the negative association you have of that place. You have now been away from there longer than you were there. Don't keep giving it power. Remember they are stories, and everything is filtered through perspective. If someone focuses only on the negative that's what they will continue to see. But you know that's not reality. You have felt safer in cities which you were told were high crime and not safe, but was that the life you were living there? No.

Remember the source. Find those who stayed who aren't seeing the bad. They choose to stay and aren't of the same mindset. Find the memories that are happy when you look back instead of the terror you lived through. You had friends and family members who helped you through. Focus on the good not the bad. Calm your mind. These are visits. Just a few days. It's not worth the weeks of mental distress you are putting yourself through. Release it. Move on.

Be careful when it's your ego self that wants to respond vs your authentic self. There is a time to speak up and a time to be the bigger person and see that it's an ego vs ego argument. You get to decide when enough is enough and when to hold your tongue. There are consequences to both. Weight them before you speak. Decide where your boundaries and priorities are and act accordingly. You have a voice too. Is that voice coming from love or coming from someplace else? This is your last interaction for this year. Where do you want to leave off with things? How do you want to roll into the new year? What changes do you or don't you want to see in your relationships? What is the holiday really about for you?

You get to decide how this weekend plays out. How do you choose to view the inconveniences you are given? Will you choose to be positive about things or will you drag yourself and the experience down? Will you make yourself sick worrying about things or stay in a higher vibration and choose health? Everything is in your hands. Be who you want to be this weekend. It's a different aspect of you. This is not your normal weekend at home. You aren't around others on a constant basis. So, choose a positive spin on your day. See how much better it feels.

Fear is often your unwillingness to set something in motion and deal with the changes that come about as a result. It sometimes sounds like "I don't want to deal with that right now". It's putting something on hold that you know needs to be addressed. Fear isn't always being afraid of something. Sometimes it's delaying the effort and work needed to move past things. You must find the courage to know the difference and act if you are to get to where you need to be. Change is not always comfortable. It's part of growth and you must release something to hold something new. Weigh the value of what you will gain and what you are sacrificing to get there. Has what you are releasing run its course? Is it pulling you down or holding you back?

Things can't always be as they are. You see that through generations of family. One generation is tight knit and stays in the same area. The next spreads its wings, tries a different lifestyle, expands, grows. Those that stay feared the changes the next generation made. There are expectations on how they were to live their lives that molded their fears and disguised them as values and traditions, but aren't they still fears, the fear of change, fear of being judged, fear of no one taking care of the generation before? Find what is fear and what is tradition. Find where fear is hiding and call it out for what it is. You don't need to face all of them but recognize when they are running your life instead of you. Have the courage to recognize and take back control. You are braver than you think.

SHADOW WORK

L et it rise to the surface until it overflows, takes over, creates a new landscape, and saturates the land. It must be released to receive its full benefit, an overwatering that then gets stored in time of need to help in the future. But it must be released to help things grow. To help you grow.

Reliving past misgivings is not a happy mind space, but to be able to forgive, sort out what had to be learned, remove the power you gave the event and take back your power, is what needs to be done. You are bringing to the surface the parts of yourself and your confidence that you gave away. You are taking back your life. You are restoring balance. You are coming full circle and nourishing your soul with that which was once poison, until you are strong again and able to withstand anything that comes your way.

Find the balance. Find the thread and pull it. Unravel it to see what is really there. What is it made of? What are you made of? How can we make it stronger, less likely to fray moving forward? How can we fix it if we don't find where the cracks are?

What can we tell you that you do not know. Do the work. Move the obstacles out of your way. You know what they are, that's part of it. Where do they come from? Heal their location. Forgive, Forgive, Forgive. It's not all your fault. You are blocking the way by stopping the flow. You start to move then get scared, fall over, and then complain that you'll never get there. Stay on your feet. Move further each time. You understand how it feels to fall, so it shouldn't be scary. Now learn how to stand, how to shine, how to be in the moment and how to stay a little longer each time, until it gets easier for you and becomes second nature like falling over was. Just shift your perspective. You get frustrated and take yourself out of the moment. You can acknowledge the frustration but stop giving it control. Let it just go by. Ignore it like a child begging for attention. It will eventually give up once you stop feeding into it.

You started to flow. You didn't lose focus. You just had an expectation that you must release. It's not always going to appear how you want when you are coming from a place of control. You need to release that need for control. It has served you but now it is no longer needed and new lessons need your focus. What are you doing to release that control? You need to learn to trust. Trust in others, in yourself, in your guides. Trust that if you let down your guard, you won't be let down or disappointed. You need to gain trust again. You lost that when you were betrayed in the past, but you have shifted who you surround yourself with and this is you giving yourself permission to be vulnerable again, to trust again, to not have expectations for failure. Can you release control and trust your instincts?

———

It's never too late, start now. It has begun, you are on your journey. You just need to stick to the path and keep going. Enjoy it. It's part of the process. This is not meant to feel like a chore. You are discovering, learning new things, and remembering what is. It should be exciting for you. It's a way to connect, to fill in the dots to create a picture of what could be.

You are letting it stress you out. You take things too seriously. Have fun with it. Enjoy life. You weren't meant to be miserable. That is not how others perceive you. That's how you view yourself. There is a disconnect there. You are in your own way and are your own worst critic. You are judging and being hard on yourself for things that are not relevant. You are giving things power that you shouldn't and then you feel drained and wonder why.

You are in a mental game for the most part. When you aren't physically doing things, you are mentally driving yourself crazy. Yes, there are concerns, but you act, and you move on. When you fixate you give away your power and you make things worse. You feel worse and the situation does not benefit or improve. You need to let go.

What are you doing with the list of things to address? Knowing what they are is great, but you still need to put in the work of releasing them or shifting how you view them. Knowing only gets you so far. Use the information you are given to improve the situation, to improve your life. Make the shifts and changes. It's quicker than you think. Let go of your expectations on how the release should be or feel. You'll just know. It doesn't have to be so cut and dry.

You are so structured and guarded. You built up this wall to prevent collapse after hitting rock bottom from not taking control, but you forgot to add windows to your walls. So, nothing is getting in, and no one is getting out. What you constructed needs to still let in light and breathe. There is a difference between a house and a prison. Which have you constructed for yourself? Do you feel safe or trapped in what you have constructed due to past circumstances? Rebuild. Make it correct for where you are now, for who you are now. Pay attention to the setting. Has the view changed and become more scenic? Focus on that view. Let in the light. Let it breathe.

Problems are only learning opportunities. Look for the solutions. You already have the answers. You just need to trust yourself. It's good to ask until you get that confidence, but the goal is to get you to trust your instinct and live life with confidence, making things happen with no hesitation and no worrying about what everyone else thinks, just living, creating, and evolving.

You are stronger than you think. Fear is still a problem. You at least know the solution is to face it or move on, but not live in it. Yes, there are things to worry about and common sense to use like not ignoring health issues. For some of the more trivial things your fear brings them into your awareness which creates them in your life. It's a constant process of sorting out what's really a threat and what is fear. Use your instinct, ask the questions, and see how the answers feel when you say them. Your body knows and will indicate which way to proceed.

Once you take care of your health you can start to use your body for what it was made for. Pick up on its signals. Know what you need to work on before it manifests into a health concern or deeper issues. You are not using your resources properly. They teach you information that is relevant to your survival but don't teach you the things that would benefit you most on this plane. Rute memorization is not learning. The information you are taught in schools is biased and limited. They are brainwashing you and you spend your life trying to sort out what's the truth or not as a result.

Stay away from politics. There are no winners when there are set parameters and decisions aren't being made for the greater good. This is just a level of frustration due to lack of control or say. There are those here assigned to reset the system but it's going to take time. You are not here for that. Let them fight their fight. You focus on yourself. It's good to be aware of what's going on but don't get caught up in it to the point where you get discouraged or lose momentum on what you came here to do.

Different degrees of the same experience, which side of the seesaw are you on? It's got ups and downs and a sliding rule. Where are you at any given point in time, in any particular feeling, emotion, or experience? You get to choose where you land and how long you stay there. Permanence is only what you allow as you need to shift and change as more information becomes available. If you stay you might get stuck and not grow, but mold.

Where are you with your life, with your responsibilities, and thought patterns? Are you addressing or becoming stagnant in your personal growth? You can't grow if you don't shine light on those things that need to change. You can't keep moving things around in the shadows and expect them to receive full exposure. You are just avoiding the growth needed. Are you planting in the wrong areas again? Are you overwatering or nourishing your life? What's taking root and what's starting to rot? Where's your accountability?

Push through. You need to keep moving. It's always another day, then another. They keep going. Are you focusing on the ones lost or the ones still to come? Are you wishing ones away looking for the more "important days", or living each day to the fullest? How are you spending your time? Are you productive or avoiding? Are you worrying or promoting change? If you can't solve one problem, move onto one you can. There is not an exact order or sequence you need to follow. You just need to keep moving forward, no matter which foot starts.

Life is what you make of it. If you aren't happy, change it. People will stay stuck and miserable in something they have complete control over and will give their power away to excuses and fears, instead of putting in the effort and work to build something different. They daydream about futures they expect to fall into their laps rather than evaluate and take control of where they are, and the steps needed to get to that dream. The only one standing in the way of your potential is yourself, and until you realize that you will continue to stay where you are because it's no one else's responsibility to live your life, it's yours. What are you doing to break the patterns and make the changes?

Awareness is the first step. You need to open your eyes first if you want to see, but you then need to lift your foot and walk if you want to get somewhere with it. Knowledge needs action to produce change. If you aren't willing to move, then you aren't going to magically appear in another scenario or stage in life. You can make all the plans you want, but they do no good if you don't implement them.

You need to find out why you aren't taking the steps needed for what you desire. What is holding you back and how do you address it? Are you talking yourself out of things, if so, where is that coming from? Could it be crystalized belief systems that were instilled by others that aren't even yours, or defense mechanisms that were set up for another life experience that isn't relevant for this one that you need to release? Why are you preventing your own greatness?

Accountability is crucial if you want to make changes. You can't keep placing blame for why you are how you are. You need to realize you have the control to adjust to most circumstances. Yes, something might have happened in your past but it's over now. Are you going to let it control your future? You give power to your experiences. You allow them to shape your life, positive or negative, but that power you gave them is your power, and you can take it back whenever you want. Where are you allocating control of your life? Who or what is behind the wheel and controlling where you are going?

When you are too busy staring at the map and trying to figure out a course, the driver has been moving you toward a different destination and you never even noticed. You need to look up from our life every once in awhile and see where you are and how you got there. Are you lost or did you take a detour? Are you out of gas or do you have what you need to get back on course? What do you need to get where you want to go? Are you setting up the directions to lead you there or are you driving around aimlessly and hoping for the best? How are you living your life? Who's driving? Where are you going? When do you plan to get there? You have more control than you think. What are you doing about it? Are you charting your course for success or are you on a racecourse going full speed in circles? The choice is yours.

Things don't always have to be as complicated as you make them. Sometimes you let the struggle define you and are not sure how to proceed with it, but there are better, easier ways to live life. You just need to be open to them. When you are closed off, you will continue to do things the hard way, not even realizing that you made that choice.

Patience is one way to find a better path. When you are able to trust, then you'll stop putting restrictions and time frames on things which will allow them to unfold in their own time. You can't rush things just to have control then wonder why your results aren't the best they could be. You need to let go, to release being so regimented in your actions. Why do you get agitated? Why can't you trust? How do we release it if we don't dig in, find it, and address it? You have set up your own boundaries of where you feel comfortable. But you aren't the same person that created those boundaries. Don't let your past dictate your future. You've outgrown those things, so you need to leave them in your past and move forward. It will feel like a weight is lifted once you release that need to control. You are safe now. You don't need the big walls around you. Use the bricks to build better things. Dismantle your past, reuse what you can, share what you've learned, but move forward.

Progress is work. If you want to see something, you must do something. Things won't always fall into your lap. You must participate in life to set things in motion if you want to see changes. It can't happen on its own. You are an active participant in life. It happens for you, not to you. However, it doesn't stop moving just because you are having a bad day. You set things in motion, and they need to continue to run their course until completion. But wouldn't you rather be a part in the direction, the speed, the fulfillment of that which you started? Take credit for your achievements. Learn from your missteps.

What are you doing today? Are you viewing everything as a chore on your list, or are you also going to live life? Find some joy, breathe the air, see the world, and interact with it. There are different types of growth, and they are all important; physical, mental, emotional, social. They all feed into the greater part of the whole. When you keep your focus on only one aspect of your life, you start to miss the value needed from the other facets of who you are. You always have the option of variety and can set your focus accordingly, so you don't burn out. If you don't feel like this, do that. If you get stuck here, move over there. You need to be in the flow, that's how the Universe works. It is not rigid. A stream flows better in curves than right angles. But it also keeps moving. There are slow spots, but there is always some part of the current moving on some level.

If you are burning out, ask yourself why. Is it because you need to step away and refocus or are you working toward the wrong things? Is this good use of your time for the life you want to live, or are you doing things out of habit and obligation? What is the point or purpose? What can be removed that is not necessary and is taking up your time? It's not that you don't have enough time. It's that you aren't using it in the best manner to serve your needs. Take a look at what you are doing. If your need to decompress is constant, then there might be something causing that need that might not be the best fit for your life.

If your job is making you miserable and is the majority of your time, you need to ask yourself, "could I pay my bills doing something I love instead?" "Can I make an effort toward that shift?" To stay in a situation that is draining you is a choice. Why are you making that choice? Why do you feel you aren't worthy of something better? Why do you feel you deserve to be treated badly? Why do you think you can't have more or be more? Why are you actually choosing to punish yourself? It's not the company or your co-workers punishing or treating you badly. It's you, treating yourself badly by choosing to stay. It's a choice. Why do you not love yourself enough to want something better and work toward it? Change is a choice. What are you doing to implement it? How do you want to live your life?

———

Find the roots. That's a good place to start. Go back to the basics. Find what drives you, what excites you, why you came on this journey in the first place. See what you missed, and what you can brush up on. See what comes up from there. Get back to the source of things. See the progress. Find your gratitude. Sometimes learning can move backwards before it can push you forward. You need to release and sometimes find the root of things to really be able to grow. Try a different path to get to the same destination if one doesn't feel right or isn't working. There are many ways to do something. It's about not getting discouraged and still moving in whatever direction you can. Learning whatever lessons help.

Reviewing what was previously taught could teach you something new because your perspective and view have evolved and changed. You will hear and receive something different as it's meeting a new version of you. It's also repeating information which helps reinforce the lessons to override any subconscious defaults that might still be holding onto views that aren't serving you. Never feel it's a waste of time to review information you are drawn to or might have heard before. It's like watching a favorite movie. You watch it enough times and you learn the script. It's the same with learning information, you listen to the same concepts and information enough it becomes a part of your life and gets incorporated into your story. Just pay attention to what you are repeating to yourself because that's the results you are asking for.

There are different methods for different results in your spiritual journey. Meditation helps with balance and connecting you to your higher self and grounding you. Affirmations and mantras help repeat the things you are trying to override in your subconscious to help fix embedded beliefs. Connecting with your guides either through channel, meditation, or visualization helps connect you to your bigger story and receive the guidance you need. Then there's your awareness which connects you to the present where all things are happening, where change can occur.

You can't just choose one and think, ok I got this. They all serve different purposes in your growth in this journey. Connect to each one according to what you are looking to work on or receive. Knowing this is half the battle and you are slowly coming into the realization of how these different aspects can help you and what they are for. Keep going. Get excited about the journey. Realize when you are falling into bad patterns. Stop and breathe and shift directions accordingly. The information does nothing if you don't turn it into action. Reading a good book does nothing if it doesn't change your life or your view in some way. Analyze and reflect on whatever comes up. Ask questions, seek results. It's ok to not have all the answers. Part of this journey is getting to the point where you know you need to ask for help or find out more. Growth can't happen without wonder, or inquiry. So, ask away. Seek to find. There is so much hidden waiting to be discovered.

To fix a broken record you must get it to stop repeating the same thing. For your development that would be resolving the negative self-talk and your old paradigms that are preventing you from grooving to the flow of your life. You must patch over the broken part, smooth out the scratch, fill it with the opposite. So, repeating something different is the only route that makes sense. You'll have to fill it in as many times as needed to get the old damage to disappear. It might seem tedious as you have gotten used to anticipating the skip and the repeat and forgot how it should sound if not for the issues, but wouldn't you love to move past that, to have life working properly, to hear the sound of success, to hear the completed pieces not just what is broken?

You didn't have to be the one that broke it to fix it. You don't need to know the cause to know the solution. You don't need to be whole to fix a small part. It's a process you learn along the way, but realizing there is an issue and accepting responsibility for fixing it is where you need to start. Create a game plan and just start. A little bit a day will go a lot further than procrastination will. You need to figure out what works for you and is easiest for you to maintain, morning, after work, before bed. Try each one if you need to but find the fit and maintain the momentum. Knowing is not the same as doing. Doing is the action that is needed to see results.

Don't feel overwhelmed when what needs to shift keeps coming to the surface. It will become less once you start the work. Right now, it's a child begging for attention. You need to give it that attention for it to be satisfied and move onto something else. Once you acknowledge it, that sets things in motion. It's like turning your computer on then walking away. The screen is still going to be active. The updates are still going to want to run whether you are sitting there or not, but you can't use your computer till all the updates are installed so you need to press continue and do the work before you can restart and see the improvements.

You understand what needs to be done. You are on the path. Keep going. It won't get easier until you start paying attention and doing what needs to be done. Pay attention to what excuses you are giving yourself and what distractions you "feel" you need to relax. What are you relaxing from? Will doing the work fix that problem as well? You are trying to change a default habit. It is going to keep trying to stay its old course. You need to be louder and fight harder to establish your dominance. Remind yourself of the end result you are shifting to, the brighter side of things once it's incorporated. You need to want it enough to push through the uncomfortableness. Change is hard but it is necessary. Keep going. Just keep going.

***

Everything is a learning process happening for you not to you. As you address certain paradigm shift things will come into play to see where you are. Don't resort back to old habits. Implement what you learned, release the thought patterns, and give control to the Universe. Be in the present. You keep filling your time with things. Learn to be ok with the silence and not doing. It's not space to be filled. It's reflection and grounding you are avoiding that needs to be done. If it feels like you are avoiding that, you might be. Notice when you do that and ask yourself why. You keep stressing yourself out, worrying about the future, judging the past, worrying about explaining yourself in imaginary stories. Why do you need to explain yourself to anyone? You owe no one a reason for where you are, what you do, or how you spend your time. You are living your life. That is going to show up however it does for where you are in the process. The only one you need to hold yourself accountable to is yourself.

You still get angry instead of just accepting those things you can't control like your sleep patterns, your finances, apartment stuff, car issues. You have immediate reactions that don't serve you. How about instead of having a reaction you pause. That's all, just start there. When something happens, pause. Then say, this is how it is. I can accept, change, or move on. Make a decision and run with it. Don't dwell, don't let your emotions drag you into a "theme" for the day. Address it and move on. Anything else is giving your power away and you need to make the decision not to do that anymore. That does not serve you and we're not doing that. Implement what you have learned and move on with your day to better more productive things. A speed bump is just that, a speed bump. It's not the main objective of the journey.

You get to decide the relevancy of the information given and incorporate or digest however you see fit. Our job is to guide. Your job is to put it into action and manifest what you need or want. We cannot do that for you. You must still do the work to see results. You aren't lost. You are just sorting out the next steps and incorporating the shifts needed to get there, but you know what you need to work on and the general direction.

You still need to trust and to have patience. Don't let negativity derail you from all you have done so far. You need to be persistent in your perspective and attitude until it becomes habitual. You are coming from years of expecting the worst and complaining in your head when you feel overwhelmed. Work on flipping that. You've already seen the results, but you have to keep at it. It doesn't come naturally to you yet, but you'll get there. Your paradigm will keep bringing you back to worry, or excuses, or looking for pity, but you don't need any of that. It eats up your time that could be better spent manifesting what you do want. Notice it sooner. Find the thought you want to use as your "go to" so you always have it ready. You need to view life in a positive light, or it will continue to feel dark. It's a habit which is why it feels comfortable, but we don't want to be comfortable. We want change.

IT'S NOT A CHORE. IT'S EVOLUTION

We want new and improved, and you need to be uncomfortable for a while until those changes are incorporated. Don't give up on yourself so quickly. You are more capable and determined than you think you are. Prove it to yourself and hold onto that feeling. You are going to need it.

You need to meditate and visualize what you want to see. You need to get in the habit of adding this into your daily routine so you can practice and get it down. You know this is where you need to work. You don't need a guided visualization. You need to visualize it in your own way, so you know what needs addressed. It doesn't always have to be guided. You need to start believing in your own capabilities if you want to start to see real results. You know what you need better than a random video does. Believe in yourself but do the work.

Focusing on the negative doesn't make it less so. It gives it attention and means to grow, and we don't want that. Notice what you say to yourself. Noice when you think you need to explain yourself to others and why. Is it their concern? No, it's yours. Give a yes or no and leave it. You don't owe anyone an excuse for why you live your life the way you do. It's your life, your finances, you know best.

Acceptance and perspective go hand in hand. Your view of things is where judgment comes from, which is what causes acceptance of a situation or event to come into play. Without judgement there is nothing to hold you back from acceptance. It's how you view things that is the issue. Where do you place value, concern, problems? Why do you want to control, change, or walk away from things?

It's the same with accepting yourself and your creations. How do you view the life you are living? Are you going to accept it or are you ready to make the necessary changes to see progress? You can accept, change, or move on. These are all choices you have for all situations in your life. If it's not something you have control over, you can change how you view it, how you prioritize it, or if it's time to walk away. Walking away is always an option. You need to evaluate why you are walking away though. Is it because you don't have confidence or faith in yourself or is this what is dragging you down which is why you need to walk away? Find your motive for decisions and question it. Find the place it's coming from.

Sometimes quitting is a positive course of action, when all else has been exhausted and no longer brings value to your life or opportunity for growth. Choose your battles, your goals, and your direction. See what aligns and what doesn't and make decisions accordingly. Choices become easier when you have a big picture in mind and know where you are going. Is this habit or helpful? You get to decide.

You can visualize things positively without being hung up on the details. It's the feelings and end result you are visualizing not the how you get there. The path from A to B is what you need to leave open. When you can't visualize because you are worried about the small details, that's where the issue is. Visualization doesn't need the small details figured out until it comes into form. Those details don't really matter and are a distraction. You need to let go some. Not everything needs to be figured out all at once. You need to have faith in what you desire. First bring it into being.

You need to be more confident in yourself and your capabilities. Just because the now does not show what you want in the positive manner you wish it to, does not mean it can't ever be prosperous and positive. When you keep focusing on what it is not you are preventing it from being what it could be. You keep viewing it as failing instead of initiating thoughts of abundance. You need to flip and stick to it. You need to release what the present shows if you want something different in the future.

It's a battle you need to take on if you are ever going to change what you see. It's a constant view change not just a few minutes here and there. You need to believe in success to have success. Find where you are holding yourself back and address it. You are not a failure. You have taken all the steps. You are in the home stretch, don't sabotage yourself now. This is when you really need to have faith and belief. You can do this.

———————————

Let things just be. There is no right or wrong or need for change. They just are. See them as they stand. This is the present and how things landed. Can you accept the present as it is, or will you view it with perspective or inquiry? Can things just be, or do you need to have a view or say? There is peace in just observing and not adding judgement, peace in accepting and just moving on. How much are you able to accept things at face value? How much do you need to control everything? Are you judging yourself for how you view the world?

Acceptance and non-judgment go hand in hand. Are you able to accept things or does your perspective have to play a role? How open and accepting are you really? Can you view things outside of yourself without emotion, without having an opinion, without thinking good or bad are necessary descriptors? You need to detach yourself sometimes and just view things as they are like you would art, with wonder, not counting brush strokes, wishing they had used different colors, made it bigger, added more. Things just are and can be complete as is without your point of view interfering. How judgmental are you? How accepting are you? Do you have an opinion on everything, or can they just be as they are, and are you judging yourself for how you view the world?

You must push through to make it to your destination. The work must be done to see results or to see change. The terror barrier is what stops you and pushes you back to your default settings, but if you keep pushing through enough times, it becomes the new default. Push through, keep going. The only one holding you back is you and how you decide to spend your time. What do you want to see manifest in your life? What is yours already that you need to claim? You could have the life you desire, that you want to live, but you need to set your course and adjust the steering. You need to make the turns and avoid the hazards. You'll get there but you first need to start. Then you need to focus on the road ahead. You can't get there if you keep getting distracted and pulling over to do other things.

Where is your focus? Set a time frame and watch how quickly the steps to take show up, how the obstacles disappear, and the things you need fall into place. Once you decide and put forth the effort things will fall in line for you, but you need to be serious. You need to be determined. You need to persevere. You don't need a new month to start something new. Every day is a new day. That's all you need. A starting point is whenever you say, "I got this, let's go". So, make it now. Start today. Your tomorrow awaits your changes.

ACTIONS EQUAL RESULTS

How can you have an abundance mindset when you come from a place of preparing for the worst?

This still comes back to trust and control. If you are preparing for the worst, you are not trusting how a situation will unfold and are trying to control if an outcome is not favorable. What you are doing is focusing energy on a negative outcome instead of being open and optimistic to favorable results. It's about shifting perspectives. It's not that you come from a lack mentality. It's that you are conditioned from having to pick up the pieces of things not working out, that you struggle to trust and not prepare for worst case scenarios. What that does is close you off from the results you want. You start not believing you could have positive, or that it's a trick, or the rug will be pulled out from under you. Until you deal with the trust and control issues, it will continue to seem like you don't have an abundance mindset because you struggle to focus on the "what if's" in a positive light.

You are worthy of growth and expansion. That is why you are here. Abundance is not a handout that needs to be earned or you need to be worthy of. It's your birth right. There is no lack in the Universe, there is just lack in your thinking and restrictions in your beliefs of self-worthiness. You need to remove those boundaries, open the door to opportunities and abundance, and start to accept that you can have the life you want to live. You just need to step out of your own way. Realize where you are holding yourself back and make the changes to start living to your highest potential.

You need to realize what you are doing. You can't stand in front of a closed window and wonder why there is no breeze. You need to change the circumstances to see different results. Complaining or throwing a pity party leaves you still in the same scenario. What are you doing to fix this? You need to trust in yourself, in the Universe, and in your inherent worth. Until you love yourself and know you deserve good you will continue to draw problems to yourself. You can't think negatively and be surprised when that's what you receive as that's what you planted the seeds for.

Wouldn't it be nice to not feel in shock when good things come your way, and instead know you deserve it and that is how it should be. Not entitlement but knowing you are worthy. This is how life should be as you are grateful and in flow with all that is around you. Abundance is part of you and is here to assist you in helping others and for the greater good of all you are connected to. Abundance is an opening for expansion, and you are bigger than you think you are.

Pay attention to your daydreams. Do you see abundance as temporary and sporadic or as a constant in your life? Do you cut yourself off after a dream saying that will never happen or do you leave the door open to the possibility? You are the creator of your reality. What are you opening or locking doors for? What are you willing to welcome into your life?

Expect the unexpected. You can't plan everything. It leaves no room for surprises and new experiences. It's good to have goals and a focus but you need to be open to something more than you can imagine. You limit yourself when you are too rigid or focused on specific outcomes as it doesn't allow for deviations or magic to occur. How much more exciting would it be to aim for one thing but receive so much more than you ever could have imagined for yourself? Reach beyond what you already know is possible. Dream bigger than you think you can achieve. Leave room for infinite possibilities and allow yourself to receive more.

You don't even realize you are limiting yourself when you are closed off to different possibilities of what your future might become. Yes, have a direction and things you want to accomplish but that does not mean you stop once you achieve it, as it might just be a stop on your journey not your destination. What if you could be so much more? Are you going to stop and not be curious? Are you open to possibilities or closed off because it's not part of *your* plan?

Be aware of how often you impose limitations on yourself and stop reaching, and when you stop mid accomplishment not realizing you could have more than what you are grasping for. It's like a dark hole you put your hand into and if you just reached further, you'll find the button that opens the wall and a hidden room of potential outcomes. You just need to reach further to gain more. Never stop pushing yourself. Don't let others or your own self-doubt prevent you from the greatness just over the horizon.

———————

Where do we go from here? You just keep going. Stopping is only a delay on the journey. Time and the Universe will keep moving regardless of your participation. You can move with it or fight it. The choice is always yours. Do you want progress or stagnation? You need to decide and own up to the consequences of that decision.

How many times can the same lessons be taught, the same message be given, and information received before it gets incorporated or makes a difference? You have to want to change, be driven for success. Prioritize yourself in your life instead of the mindless tasks that currently take up your time.

You have the game plan, but you need to implement and set new habits to start to see results. What do you want to see, more of the same or new and different results? You are in control of everything you see and experience. What are you allowing? Why and what are you gaining from it? It's much too easy to get caught up in doing the same as you've always have, but that's you allowing a rut. That's you stopping, instead of making progress. Why are you selling yourself short? Do you not see your potential? Do you not know your worth? You could have so much more, be so much more, but you keep giving up on yourself. You need to recognize this and find out why.

You are here to do great things. Don't sell yourself short. Take the steps toward something new and see yourself bloom. You were meant to shine.

———

It's a full circle. Come around. Repeat what you need to until it makes sense, until you have learned it, until you see the details, meaning. and lessons, never ending patterns or a pause, release, and new direction making progress on a new path. The choice is yours. How aware are you of the shapes and patterns you create, or the dreams or nightmares you choose to live? You choose the path and how it runs. Are you running toward something, away from something, or are you choosing to stay stuck?

Come over the hump, over the horizon. Start a new day, a new life. You just need a starting point to go in a new direction, but you still need to move, to motivate, to take steps. Will they be forward or are you going backwards trying to fix a past that is gone, that is not broken, just over? The lessons were learned. You are a different person now. There is nothing you need there. So, let it rest in peace and you live. You move. You dream. Move into the future with your head held high ready for whatever will come your way, knowing that it is a better place than where you have been.

IT'S NOT A CHORE. IT'S EVOLUTION

You can only live in the present. Everything else is remembering or building, but all progress happens here in the now, at this time. You have the future in your hands. Will you build it or keep delaying it, busying your time with tasks and regrets about your past? You are the bricklayer. What are you building? How bad do you want it? How quickly do you want to see the foundation laid? How quickly do you want to see results and live your new life? This is all decided now. What do you choose?

You are in charge of you, no matter your obligations. Ultimately you can still go or not go, do or not do. These are personal choices and come down to your commitment, or lack thereof, toward what you are supposed to be doing with your time. You always have the option to call in sick from work, cancel plans, choose something else. It comes down to awareness that your time is not actually set in stone. Once you realize this you can take back control of your life and make different choices or hold yourself accountable for the life you "choose" to live. At the end of the day, whatever you did that day, you chose to do.

Routines are tricky. Once you do something enough you go into auto-pilot because it is now your default and where you feel comfortable. However, you forget, it wasn't always a routine. It was new once too and you had to get used to it to make it a routine, to make it a default, from your work hours, your commute, when and where you run your errands, that show you like to watch in the background. They were all new things you turned into routines. You can just as easily set new goals, new habits, new routines. You just need to be committed enough to do the same thing enough that it becomes comfortable, becomes habit. You can change what these things are at any time. You started them. You can change them.

Take back control of your life. Realize how you got where you are and make decisions on what you do or don't want to see in the life you are building. Awareness is the key to opening your eyes and clearly seeing your creations and what you are capable of. You can change what doesn't work. Take back control of your life. This is your creation.

Obligations disappear once awareness sets in, and you realize everything is an option. There are consequences to the choices you make but your obligations are ultimately choices. Are they your choices or imposed by others? Are they beneficial to where you are going and the life you want to live, or are they busy work to fill someone else's bucket? How do you really want to spend your time? What would you rather be doing? You need to be mature enough to realize you are in charge and can change whatever does not suit you. You are past the point of being a kid where parents and teachers make your decisions. Did you continue that theme by putting bosses and spouses in charge of you, or have you broken free and started building your own life? Who's really in charge here? Who created the life you are living now? Is this what you want it to be?

There needs to come a point where you take accountability for where you are and make decisions for your future. Now that you see how you got here, you get to decide if you stay or if you adjust your path to where you want to go. Who's really in charge? Is it fear, inadequacies, other's views of how they think you should live your life? Who's in charge of you? And if it's not yourself, why is that and how can we fix it? Be mature. Be aware. Be the project manager of your life and bring the job to completion. You are building your future. Don't you want to see how beautiful it could be?

Push through. Keep going. Don't stop. Life does not slow down waiting for you to catch up. Time keeps on passing, opportunities expire, things change. You need to move with the flow or be left behind. It's a game of double-dutch. You need to know when to jump in and take your turn otherwise you are just a spectator not a participant. You can't keep calling out sick in your life. Maybe you are sick of your current life and the cure is progress, commitment to a new one, to the changes needed for things to improve. How tethered are you to where you are now? Are you willing to cut the strings once you take flight, or will you choose a safety net over soaring freely? How much do you trust in what you are building? What do you need to feel confident enough to make a move?

You know what you need to work on, yet you hold yourself back from doing the work. Is the how not clear or are you not ready? What is the problem? You can't solve it if you don't know what it is. You can't move forward if you don't lift your feet and go. You need to stop putting your life on the back burner. You can't be that scared little girl forever. You already rescued her from that environment. You have already proved you can support yourself. You know who will help you if something goes wrong. Everything is set up. You just need to start. You don't even need to wait for a signal. This is at your own pace. You aren't in a competition, but you won't get to the end if you don't pick up your pace. It's time for progress. Let's go.

What doesn't bend breaks. You need to be able to adapt and change as new information becomes available, new lessons are learned, new ideas surface. It does not mean abandoning what you were working on but adjust it accordingly so that the progress and steps make sense. If you are too busy controlling and being set in how you think things should be, you'll miss the shortcuts, the aha moments, and the tweaks that will make it better. How flexible are you? Change is part of life. If you can't incorporate it, then you will be stuck where you've always been. Don't you want to grow and expand? Life doesn't need to feel like a routine. Each day can be different. It's all choices and changes you are or aren't willing to make that set up the life you are living. How set are you on this being how you want to live your life? You can change it whenever you are ready. You can bend, shift, and change routes.

Your feet aren't firmly planted. Sometimes they need to be ready to run or move, to react to what's really happening, but your eyes need to be open first. You can't see what's happening when your eyes are closed. You need to have an awareness. You need to be willing to move at any given time, to head to something better, more inline with the direction you want to go, not more of the same. Are you prepared to be flexible or are you rigid and at a breaking point? You get to choose. Unclench your jaw. Loosen your shoulders. Let go of what is tensing you up and make room for something better. Collapse and build something new.

––––––––––

You can overdo almost anything: from sleep, sugar, negative thinking, coffee, tv, or complaining. Not all things are bad, but in excess there could be problems. Restraint comes with awareness. How aware are you of your habits, good or bad? How aware are you of the holes you dig for yourself due to lack of self-restraint? Do you know when to say when, when you've had enough, or do you keep going out of habit? You need to be aware of what you are doing and why. Are your habits actually serving you or bringing you down? Where could you better serve yourself? What could you cut back on to make life easier? You get to make these decisions. But you need to realize what you are doing before you can make a conscious effort to change things. Are you running the show or are you in default mode going through the motions?

What do you want to see in your life? Are your actions leading you to it or away from it? Are you set up for success or failure? What are you doing to fix the problems, or do you not see them as problems yet? How do you see your life and how do you want to see it? Where can we make adjustments to get those to align? You get to make the choices that change that gap. How aware are you of what's happening and how you live your life? How determined are you to change? Do you really want to see your dream life, or are you ok with living this one on repeat?

Find the peace within yourself and come back to that when you need to. You are an overthinker and tend to prepare for the worst as a need to control negative outcomes, but you are setting yourself up for stress and fixated on the negative, bringing it to you sooner. You need to shift quicker and realize when you are doing this. Find a happy thought or a positive goal you want to retreat to when you are pulling yourself down. Remind yourself of where you really are which is firmly planted. Bring that optimism into the day with you. Believe good is coming your way. Be patient about the when. Know you are on the up and up and go with that flow.

You can't be negative then wonder why negative finds you. Come out of your cocoon and spread your wings. You aren't sure what you should be doing so you do nothing. Try something. Experiment. When you are being creative or accomplishing things, your mind is open, and ideas and direction have a way to enter. Don't live your life distracted. That's not really living. That's just passing time. Don't look back at this time as years wasted. Make attempts to change. See what you can do. You don't need finances to set the groundwork up or to dream and set a plan. There is always progress to be made.

Don't keep convincing yourself that you are drained. You are just unmotivated. Find a direction that is pulling at you and go with it. There are no wrong steps. Everything is either progress or learning. Your days are open to you. Use them for your future. Be optimistic about your future not down about where you are financially now. That's just a temporary condition that can change at any time. But you need to put in the effort, mentally and physically. Get into the right mindset and see how your day unfolds from there.

Obligations don't have to be negative. It's all how you want to view it. If you are viewing it as a restriction or preventing you from doing something else then the problem isn't that you have an obligation. It's just an obligation that does not fit how you want to live your life. So, you must ask yourself why is this prioritized? Is it necessary? Either cancel it or change your perspective of it. If it serves no value, it should not be on your schedule. You don't owe anyone else your time. It is yours and you get to determine how it is spent and the consequences of proceeding or cancelling. You are never really stuck. Being stuck is a state of mind and is the result of lacking direction, conviction, or motivation.

Commitments can be beneficial if they serve you and where you are taking your life. It can be viewed as a validation of progress, an assurance from another, or a firm step toward accomplishing your goals. Everything is how you view it, how you prioritize things, and how you prefer to spend your time. You need to bring your awareness to what is inline or not inline for your goals. Being dedicated to a cause is not a bad thing if that cause is relevant to your life and your choices are yours and not to appease another. Look at how these items got on your calendar. What is the reason? What are the benefits or downfalls? Whose life are you living, your own or are you putting on a façade trying to appease someone else? Look at what's really happening. Open your eyes. It's not a cancellation. It's a realization.

Be at peace with where you are today, how far you have come and what you have been through. You cannot change how you got here but you can be grateful for the destination and your perseverance to be here in this moment, under these circumstances. You don't often notice the effort or changes you have made along the way that directed your course, but you have steered yourself to this moment and you should be proud.

There doesn't need to be a milestone or a completion of something to be proud of where you are. Just choose an aspect of your life for comparison to how you felt about it in the past and see how that dictated the better choices and better outcomes you are living in now. Take time to be grateful for where you are and who you have become. Life is full of learning experiences, and you have incorporated and learned from them instead of constantly repeating. Some don't make it out of the repeating loop. Awareness has allowed you to take ownership and direct your path toward a better future. You choose not to stay blind to what's happening and see what could be done instead.

Be content with where you are today knowing that it's an improvement from where you were. It doesn't need to be the end of improvements but validate yourself for the work you put in and where you landed. Find joy and celebration in your life at this moment. You can choose to focus on the good or the bad. Which feels like a better use of your day? Be grateful and be kind to yourself. You can only find peace when you accept yourself and where you are.

RUTS AND STAYING MOTIVATED

What is to come? Acceptance is what is to come. You are building something new. When something is new, it's not been here before so trying to fit it into the confines of expectations won't work. You need to be open, willing to see things differently, to experience something you are not familiar with. You need to grow, to expand.

You can't make progress if you are only rearranging or repeating the familiar or what is comfortable for you. Everything was new and uncomfortable at first, then you learned, added it to your routine, and it became familiar, a part of you. It must start somewhere. You are here to evolve not walk around in circles.

You need to be open and not worried, not looking for the downside or the problems before you even begin. That's where your hesitations and fear come from. If you would just stay in the present and experience things as they come without judgement but with curiosity, you would enjoy life so much more. What you would gain out of experiences would be so much more.

Step into the light. Move into your new life, make it your own. Set it up how you like, but you still need to move forward to step into it. You can't stand outside the door admiring what could be but never opening the door and becoming. Don't worry about how your future might look to others. There are no *others* we are all connected. You will start to see who supports your betterment and who lives in fear or in a need to control others to fill a void in their lives. However you must remember, it's your life to live, not theirs. They have their own story and book to write, but you get to be the main character in the one you are writing for yourself. What type of character and adventures are you going to give yourself?

All steps are important no matter how small. It builds up and you start to get excited about the possibilities. A rut is only available when you stop moving and stop trying. When stopping to catch your breath has you setting up shop in the woods instead of continuing on the path, that's when you start to get frustrated. If you get impatient you will never make it to your destination. Don't give up on yourself. Keep going. The sun will eventually shine through the trees, the path will clear. You will come to an opening, a greater expansion of what you could be. You just must keep taking steps forward.

Clear your mind and connect. That's all you need to do. Then pay attention and don't get in the way. Your need to control or overthink is what blocks you. You worry about the wrong things and default to feeling you are a failure before you even try. You give up on yourself so quickly. You need to believe in yourself and your inherent gifts and connections. Once you let go of your negative mindset it will start to feel more natural but for now you are almost fighting who you believe yourself to be instead of focusing on who you really are. You need to shift and believe.

You can only get so far when you are holding yourself back from progress. You need to be in the present moment. You need to see the possibilities. You need to make different choices if you want to see different results. You aren't stuck, you have just stopped. You just need to refocus and pick up your feet and keep going. It's not that hard. You just lose motivation a lot more often than you'd like. You need to address that.

You are starting to come into better awareness and starting to take action steps to address some of the issues. Don't be scared. Go into it knowing that whatever happens needs to happen. Relax and just do what you need to do. You can't be scared of change or resolving issues. You need to fix things in order to connect and move forward properly. You need to set boundaries. You aren't a victim. Set boundaries.

You need to start viewing things as fun and not obligations. You can't constantly be frustrated with everything you need to attend or do. Yes, regulate things but don't just cancel because you don't feel like it. There's a difference between it being a bad idea and you changing where your comfort zone is. You need to get back out there and find the joy in life again. You are stuck in endless routines, which makes you lose your spark and your joy in life. Things are going to be different but that's part of life. You need to adapt and move through it.

Don't be so hard on yourself all the time. You are forgetting to love yourself. You are forgetting to forgive strangers when they are doing something that inconveniences you. You are losing your joy. You are the one people see as a spark of inspiration and you can't be that if you spend your down time miserable. Fix things. Don't just assume they will get better after this event or this thing. Those are temporary. You need to incorporate what you learn into your daily life to receive the most benefits. You need to be the change. If you aren't happy that is on you. You know how to solve it, so get to work.

Just keep moving. The blanks will be filled in as you go. You know what you need to work on so place your focus there. You need to learn to trust. It's not that you are roaming around aimlessly, you are working on what needs handled before the next transition in your life. You are between events and doing the work that is needed currently. Patience and focus are your two takeaways. Just handle what you need to work on and trust the rest will fall into place in due time. It can't always be immediate progress without doing the work. You are in the work stage of things so focus on that for now.

The frustration comes from not feeling in control but that's one of those things you need to work on. If you trusted more, you would worry less. You still need to work on letting go and surrendering. That's where you will find peace and balance. You still have this vision of what you feel should be happening when you aren't doing the work for that. Just let it go. It's ok to not have a firm idea of what's next. It will keep you from stressing about it or trying to focus on results. It also prevents you from distractions as you work on the shadow work that needs to happen. You are taking steps even if you aren't sure what you are doing. Progress is being made; awareness is growing.

Reflect within. You still aren't meditating and connecting in that way. It's a large part of why you feel off balance. You aren't even practicing or connecting to the frequencies much. Put your focus on connecting and making that part of your routine as well. It's good to take steps and get the work done but there are a few steps you are forgetting that would help how you feel.

You are becoming more sensitive to energies and trying to stay balanced when those are bombarding you. It is difficult if you don't work on balancing and grounding yourself. Worry about the current transitions not those that haven't happened yet. This is where you can start to make changes and see results. You need to let go of the need for results as validation. You don't need outside sources to validate you. You need to find inner peace and self-love still. You are still worried about how things look to the outside world when this is all about an inner journey. This is why you need to focus on the present and why the work you are doing now is important. You can't help others if you can't even understand or help yourself. Make the time and go within and find out why are still struggling with loving yourself. It's the first step to connecting properly. Do the work. Forget about the results. Validate yourself first.

Life should not be constant to do lists. There is a lot to keep track of but there should be time for living in the moment and experiencing life, not just going through the list of obligations. It has shifted through life as more responsibilities are acquired, or specific changes or goals are in process. However, if you can't find joy or be in the moment then you are missing something of value. Analyze and step back every once in a while and see the importance of what you are giving your time to. Are you going through the motions? Are those someone else's values or priorities handed down? Are you doing things for you or for someone else?

If you don't start asking the questions, then you'll never know what can be adjusted to make room in your life for living it. Think about your grandparents, how did they fill their time in their early years' vs later in life? The tasks are not the same or as often. Some stopped being obligations long ago. Things often become habits and we don't even realize them until we step back and start questioning them. You don't do deep cleaning of your apartment as much as you did when you lived with other people. You don't even have a set schedule for taking out the garbage. Things change when the environment and circumstances change. There is no right or wrong, but it shows adjustments can happen and you will still be ok in life. You just need to bring things into review sometimes.

The problem is when you are evolving you want to be in that next stage, and it makes the current stages and routines seem like obligations as you know at some point, they will be obsolete or shifted and you have to keep allocating time you'd rather spend on what you want to do. It becomes disheartening, but you aren't at the next level and it's not time yet. So, you need to find the balance or a way to accept and maybe find joy in what is currently in your life. Remind yourself that once it's gone, it's gone. So maybe be in the moment with it now while it's still here instead of wishing for the future to arrive.

You lack gratitude for the things currently providing you with the life you live, even if it's not ultimately staying, is important and necessary for where you are now. To constantly think negatively of it doesn't change the present. It just makes it more unbearable for you. You need to let it go. Find the patience and joy you once had. At one point this was a step up to get you to where you were going. View it with appreciation for all it has provided. It did not do anything wrong or different. You were the one that changed, not your job, just your priorities. Don't get upset at things being what they always were when your perspective is what is shifting the view. Enoy the present. Find some joy. Accept that it won't be here forever and appreciate it being here now.

<hr>

Move forward toward something. Standing still will get you nowhere. You need to be open to change, to stepping away from what you know, to being uncomfortable. If you only go after what makes you comfortable, you'll never see your true potential or how far you can really go. What are you afraid of? What is it that causes you to hesitate? Why are you holding yourself back?

Don't get distracted by the problems. Focus on solutions and lessons that it might be teaching you. Move on from things. Don't let them drag you down with them. You can't throw something away and still follow it to the dumpster. You need to detach quicker and find the direction you are supposed to be going and get back to it. You are only holding yourself back when you get wrapped back up in inconveniences and let them set the tone for you and your progress for the day. Just view it for what it is, a problem that needs attention. Give it that attention and then move forward.

Though you do need to sit with your emotions to validate them, there is a difference between validating and wallowing or sharing your frustration and reliving it by complaining. You are keeping it alive longer, giving it fuel. You are giving it residency instead of a guest pass. Let it visit but send it on its way. Don't give it more value or power than is needed. Shift, live in the good feelings. Focus on what you can do and what feels right. You might have a lot on your plate, but each thing is only a part of your time. Be in the moment with things. Don't worry or feel overwhelmed. If you just felt things in the present, you would be fine. It's when you want to think of everything all at once that creates the overwhelm, when you want to worry about what has not happened yet, what has already happened, or worst-case scenarios, is when you get lost. Let that all go and just be present. If you get overwhelmed, come back to your breath, or choose something positive to focus on. Don't let your emotions ruin your day. They can change at any point. Be aware of what's happening.

Be aware of what you are doing. Where do you find comfort? What makes you feel safe? What are you called to in times of stress? Is it beneficial or does it make things worse? Do you wallow or release? Do you complain, distract, or move on? Stress is not your home, as familiar as it might feel. You don't need validation or a pity party. Work on stopping yourself from diving in headfirst and making it worse or living in it longer. Don't make it worse than it is by preparing for backlash that might not even be coming.

It's hard to not constantly look at the ground suspiciously when you are used to the rug being pulled out from under you. However, you need to hold your head high, trust, and see what is in front of you to make any headway. Trust that you aren't the same person that would fall flat on their face when things shift. You are more aware now. You are putting better out there to get better back. Your focus is shifting. Trusting is just the next step to building the life you want. You can't be confident in what you are building if you are worried about the foundation collapsing. Know that it is strong. Know that you built it right and move ahead with the rest of the build. You need to believe in yourself and what you have done so far and where you are going. Things happen for a reason. Is it to test where you are with things? Is it to lead you to a new, better path? Be patient and see how things unfold. You don't need to have it all figured out to keep moving. So just keep taking steps firmly in your belief that the ground is still firmly under you.

Knowing and actually doing are two separate things. When are you going to prioritize action and progress? Time keeps on moving forward, are you moving toward a new future or more of the same? The bad/Lazy days are piling up with no motivation toward goals. Break out of that cycle. Find something to do directly after work to flip your mood and reset your evening. You can't carry that funk into your free time and claim to be free.

There's a realization that you are wasting time but no action to change that. You have your moments and your bright ideas but then it fades, and you are back where you started. You know you can change. You are capable of changing and fixing habits. Don't overwhelm. Choose one and stick to it. You know where you are stuck and where the focus should be. Find a method or exercise that you can stick to for attacking that obstacle. If you don't set up a game plan you won't be able to hold yourself accountable, which is where you fall short. Set a time frame and take things seriously. Do the same for what you need to address and stick to it. You've known these blockages are there. It's time to flip them, to take back your life, to erase the negativity and self-doubt. Invest in your future. Stop talking yourself out of your potential. You are worth it, and we want to see you succeed.

You need to be excited about life again, about making the changes needed to create what you want to see. When you lose your steam or enthusiasm your new future sits in wait unable to manifest. You can't keep pushing life aside. It must be lived. You must learn to prioritize your future and the steps needed to get there. Your motivation waivers throughout the day. You need to learn how to push through that and stick to it.

These are only speed bumps not concrete blocks preventing entrance. Roll over them and keep going. You are the only one preventing your own greatness. Don't you want to see where your new destination is and what you could be doing with your life instead? Once you arrive, you are going to wonder why you didn't do this sooner. Don't give yourself a reason to look back with regret. Push through, persist. This is your future, your life. Don't you want to see it improve? You need to resolve what is holding you back. You need to see yourself as successful and capable of more. Remember that you weren't meant to live someone else's goals only your own. Leave the comparisons to others go. It does no good and slows you down. You are drawn to your spiritual life for a reason. Connect the dots. See the bigger picture. We are creating a masterpiece here. Be the artist you were always meant to be.

Change is ahead. Be open to it. Things can't keep going as they are. You are setting some things in motion and opening yourself up to new feedback and ideas. With different actions comes different results.

IT'S NOT A CHORE. IT'S EVOLUTION

When you break out of the routine you see things in a different light and can have more breakthrough moments. Meet who you need to meet. Have those conversations that bring results. Get out there and stay open to what transpires. Come at it from inspiration not just going through the motions. Things are only the same old when you are closed off to seeing them as something more. Gain what you can from situations, don't just walk around blindly. See what is really there. Be present in the moment. Things are set up for you. You just need to be awake enough to see things.

What do you want to see? If it's more of the same than that's what you will perceive, but if you are open to seeing more, you'll notice a whole other world out there. There are lessons to learn and insights to have. How closed off are you? Keep your focus and open yourself up to solutions. Notice the difference and see what comes in for you. You are creating your reality so be present in it and open your eyes. You can't walk blindly then complain when you don't see things. Come at it from a place of wonder and curiosity. Listen to what's happening around you. Take it all in. You don't need to control everything. Sometimes you just need to be present and that's enough. What will you see when you open your eyes and your heart?

How do you want to spend the weekend? What do you want to accomplish? You get to decide, but you need to push through the distractions to get there. How determined are you? Where are your priorities? You are just delaying yourself when you push things off. What are you afraid of? Why do you not see value in your progress? It's great that you know the problems and what needs to be addressed, but what are you doing to address them? You've known for a while but keep getting sidetracked. There's this place between self-care, down time, procrastination, and laziness, where you get lost. You are validating your inactivity with excuses. Are those excuses you or your ego winning out? Who's really in charge here?

You know what all you can accomplish when you focus. So why are you not focused? We're not trying to make you feel bad about how you spend your time, but we want to see you get back on track and achieve the life you want so desperately. It's easier than you think but you need to stay focused. You need to be committed. You need to prioritize your future life now or it will never come to pass. Take charge of things. Remind yourself how far you have come. See where it needs to be tweaked and adjusted. Don't let it stress you out. Just fix it and move on. Look at where your focus is. Is it on the right things? Are you viewing things negatively again? You know to be aware so adjust them. Be diligent about it. Let's move past this negative aspect and bring the positive into the light. You were meant to shine.

Attitude is everything. You can let things drag you down or you can decide to let it go and move on to better things. There's acceptance in the present. When you are just in the moment you don't need to feel or be a certain way. You can come back to your body and the present anytime life tries to overwhelm you. You are in charge of your thinking and how you react to things. Be stronger than the inconveniences or negative thoughts that come your way.

Appreciate that you can see the difference and know that none of that is real and is something you can shift or change at any time. Know that you understand how things work enough to shift whatever is not working for you. You get to choose where you go in life, how you feel about situations, and who you surround yourself with. You are never really stuck. You are either paused, need to make a change, or shift how you are viewing things.

IT'S NOT A CHORE. IT'S EVOLUTION

Take control of your life, what you see, how you feel, and where you are headed. This is your creation. Make it how you want it. Don't just sit back and let the default programing run its course. You'll miss your turns if you let the car drive itself. Open your eyes. Be present. See what is going on and get to where you are going. There's no time like the present to start a journey. It's time to hit the road.

The straight path isn't always the correct path. Easy isn't always better. It's an avoidance of things, an unwillingness for adventure, or lessons, or change. Picture it as a road under construction. If you only know that one route from point A to B, you could be sitting in traffic wasting time. But if you turn onto a side road you could find a route around the back up. You could find new places to visit, a quieter commute, a new choice or opportunity. All you need to do is try something different to find a solution to a problem.

You aren't stuck. You just need a different perspective or solution to get around the obstacle. You need to be open enough to know when it's time to try something else, and brave enough to take those steps, and commit to them. You can't keep doing what you are doing and expecting change to happen. You need to make a change to see a change. This can be set in motion by any number or things from how you spend your time, where you go, who you talk to, or what you overhaul in your life that is no longer working. You need to be aware and then you need to commit to what you want to adjust.

Take back control of things. Be brave. Be wise. See what life could really be if you took a detour and made your own path instead of following what was set out for you, or the same old path you've always taken. See what else is out there that could make life easier, more fun, or add to what you are starting. All you need to do is make a decision, put on your blinker, and take a chance.

Fear can come from unfamiliarity, anything out of your normal routine, a change, a question you don't already know the answer to. It's not a valid fear, though most fears aren't valid. Fear of the unfamiliar is not as difficult to overcome as fear of something deemed dangerous. Pushing through and completing something new is an easy resolve. Remind yourself that you can do anything, and all you have already overcome, and it will become smaller. Break it down into smaller tasks and it becomes manageable.

Change and new experiences don't have to be scary. They can be exciting. They can be tests or validations of how capable you are and how open you are to opportunities that come your way. You can't have different if you don't do different, and unless you incorporate new things or experiences, you won't be able to grow or stretch your boundaries or limitations. Those boundaries and limitations were not yours at birth. You were meant to be limitless and set those yourself for a multitude of reasons. Some valid at the time but they can always be reviewed and updated for where you are now and the direction you are headed.

Are you putting barricades on your own road to success? Are you slowing down progress, stopping the flow of things? What is in your way and how easily can it be removed? How willing are you to change directions and explore new paths? Find where you are stalling and see how valid it is. Whose excuses are you using and where did they come from? You have places to go, and fear is not your navigation system, courage is. Take a deep breath and proceed. You'll like the destination.

Circumstances might not always be to your liking but don't let it dictate your day or view of what is possible. Keep a positive outlook despite what might try to drag you down. Remember your perception is yours and you can change it to reflect what you want to see in the world. Be optimistic despite setbacks. Push through. Persist. It is the start of your day not the end. Set the tone for possibilities. If you must view a circumstance negatively, view it as your only setback and be optimistic that the road ahead is now clear.

Though you can't choose what presents itself, you can choose how you let it affect you. Don't give up your power, your time, or your day to a mild inconvenience. There is more to gain from the day through participation and outlook. Remember you are a light to shine the way for others. Don't come to the stage dim and flickering due to lack of sleep. Turn it up till it's so blinding that you have no choice but to be awake to man the lighthouse of your soul.

You don't always have to have questions to receive answers. Be open to what needs to be conveyed to you. There is growth in realizing your limited view on this plane may not provide you with the most valuable advice as your questions might have you as small, whereas your resources are infinite. Be open to what comes through. Reflect and see how best to incorporate. If you don't understand something, then set it aside until it makes sense. Answers might be for the future you, after a few more steps have been accomplished, but do go and see what's available. Express your gratitude for your resources and support.

––––––––––––––––––––

Find your niche, your flow, and move with it. Don't get caught up in what is happening around you. Stay focused and move forward. Find a way to work within your means, your grasp, and stick to it. There is a difference between working in abundance and taking unnecessary risks. What is the value or importance of things? Are they necessary or excess desires? Qualify things and notice how you feel. There is a time and a place so just be patient. That time will come. You aren't there yet.

Be grateful for where you are and what's ahead. Notice how things fall into place and aren't letting you get into a bad situation. Ask and you shall receive. You have not hit rock bottom. You had faith and it was rewarded. Keep a positive outlook and positive will come your way. Believe in an outcome and don't be surprised when it happens. The Universe will work with you, but you need to control your mind and focus and be dedicated to your goals and what you are looking for. You can't place one brick then walk away and act surprised that nothing got built. You still need to do your part. It's teamwork. If you aren't clear, then the direction isn't clear. Stay focused. Find what you need to have the exercise work and make sense to you. You are in a special time where resources are accessible to help you with anything you want to learn to do. You just need to put in the effort to find what you need, and it will appear. What are you looking to do? How much belief do you have in the outcome? Address your worthiness and see what shifts with it. Face a fear and other fears will leave with it. Start today. Carve out the time. See the results.

———

Stop holding yourself back and coming up with excuses. You are the stop light in your own life impeding the flow of traffic, creating congestion. Give yourself permission to go, move forward, make progress, get to a destination even if it's just a pit stop along the way. It's still further than where you started. This is not the time for caution. The coast is clear. Proceed. Make Haste. You have places to go, people to see, a new life to live.

You have a full tank and have prepared for this. Be excited about it. Feel the anticipation. It's a new journey, new scenery. It's not the same old. You aren't in autopilot. Pay attention to where you are going, the turns, not just the destination, all the little things along the way. Look down and see how far you have come, not how far you have left to go. Focus on the new life you are building, the sigh of relief when you've made it. The celebration and excitement of your accomplishments.

Focus on the end result and where you want to see yourself and set your course. This is your life, your road trip. You are the map maker. You create your destination with your mind, your dreams, your goals. Add in some adventure. Add in some joy. It's never a straight boring ride. Where do you want to go? What do you want to see? When do we leave? The light has turned green, Accelerate.

LEARNING AND SHIFTING

B reathe. Push past frustrations, doubt, and the need to control. These are the lessons to work on. How do you plan to address these things we need to adjust? Have you sorted it out yet? The advice needs to be used if it is to be of value. It can't just sit in a notebook on a shelf somewhere. Use what you have learned and apply it. Make progress. If that is what you want to see, then you need to make the time and effort. Not a chore but becoming something more. You can't expect progress and just stand still waiting. You can't keep focusing on the past and think you are moving forward. You are making yourself dizzy trying to sort things out in a way that is not fruitful because you forgot how to be in the flow with the Universe. You need to stop and breathe, not get angry and berate yourself or your mind for being stuck. Apparently, that is not working for you so change it. Yes, you are catching your thoughts when they go astray, but something is still finding comfort in the complaints, in the stories, in the lower vibrations. What is it that is holding you there? Release it so you can move forward.

Change takes time when you are building a new framework. You aren't just having a new idea; you are building a new life. You are adjusting to living in a new vibration. You need to be open and willing to make the uncomfortable changes when it is time to let things go and step into the light. You are still hiding in the shadows for some reason. It's not a blanket. It's not protecting you. It is holding you back from getting where you need to be. Be aware of this and when you stop out of fear and not self-care. There is a difference. You can't build momentum then get scared when you reach the speeds that will get you there. You need to push through the uncomfortableness.

On we go, onward and upward keep moving, keep going. You'll get there. Forward motion is the game. As long as you take the steps, you'll make progress, make your mark. You're doing that expectations thing again. Maybe everything doesn't need to be figured out and dissected. Maybe it can still have some magic and just be how it is, perfect without being a lesson or something you are suspicious of.

Of course, there are lessons but if you spend your time looking at things that way, you'll stop living and no longer enjoy the journey. It's not always a puzzle. You don't need to make the pieces fit. Sometimes you need to just be present and that's enough, no ulterior motive. Just breathe and be here now. Now is when everything happens. The rest has been done already and the future is changing constantly due to your choices and free will. You can change your perspective and view of the past but not necessarily the events.

Change yourself, change your direction, your destination, the speed at which you get there. We can only control so much. We are almost as reactive as you are with what we can help you with as you are the storyteller. We are just providing the props and the extras to keep it moving along. You still need to take accountability for what you create. Even when you aren't doing anything, you are creating that for yourself. You are denying another scenario that could be unfolding.

Yes, rest if you need, but when you overload in your current life and don't put steps into the one you need to build, don't be surprised when you are still in your current situation months from now. It's not going to unfold on its own. As much as you are in the learning stage between events, you still need to be doing the work as it affects the timeline of the milestones you need to hit.

If you feel behind in where you are, make a routine, adjust your focus. Make sure you are allocating some time, no matter how little, to the future you are building. As you work on it, you are living in the vibration of it, and building it exponentially at the same time. No effect goes unseen. We see how your daydreams shift when you get excited about something. Let's get that excitement going forward on what we are building so that you can get a feel for it, so you are motivated for this new life. Let's make it happen. Let's put in the work. Let's get out of the rut and make a difference. Give it your focus and attention and see what unfolds.

The present is where you create the future. But to create involves action and doing. Change cannot happen without steps being taken. Which direction are you headed? What are you creating? What type of future do you want to see and how quickly do you want it to develop? This is where your focus should be. Live in the present to create your future. Learn from the past. Learn then move forward. That's the only direction you can really make a difference in.

Every day you have decisions on how to allocate your time. It does make a difference. It affects the speed of your goals coming into view. If you don't' like where you are now, then be aware of what steps you are taking to change that. Complaining doesn't solve problems, action and perspective do. How are you spending your time? Are you fixing or standing still wallowing? You are the creator of the life you see. No one else signed your lease, accepted your job, stayed in your relationships, surrounded themselves with your friends. This is what you built. Are you proud or concerned? Are you happy or do you need to adjust some things? You put yourself here. You can leave or change it at any time. Take accountability for yourself. Be aware of how you got to where you are. Show gratitude for how far you have come. Some people never acknowledge that they can change their lives. You at least know that. So, what are you going to do with that information? Knowledge means nothing if you don't incorporate it into your life or act.

Learning is one person's point of view being dictated to another. It's information they feel is important but might not even be relevant. As with all classes, you need to use your own judgement on what is relevant, or truth, or useful in your life. Compiling other's prioritized information doesn't serve a purpose if it doesn't hold value, truth, or relevance to you. Be warry. Keep what works, discard what doesn't. Not all information is truth for everyone. This is why you are drawn to certain topics and not others. Are you listening to learn or to understand someone else's point of view? No one has all the answers, everything is filtered through their experience and past research that make sense to them at a given time. The searching is part of the journey, finding new ideas, thoughts, ways to understand or attack a situation. The value is assigned by you.

You are on a path of enlightenment. Others might also be on that path but are taking a separate route to get to their destination. Share your thoughts. They don't have to be the same. Find comfort in how much is out there to direct you and keep the wonder alive. Find what matches, be curious about what's different. See what excites them and why it's part of their path. It's not a who's right or wrong, it's about moving past what you currently see and being curious about that which you don't know is there. Enjoy those conversations of discovery. It builds your curiosity, and it keeps you moving toward something. It's much more interesting than talking about the weather or your physical jobs, or health. There is more to life out there.

You are still hiding behind the bars of your own prison. You know that you are but still you stay. Why is that? What is stopping you?

How much of it is excuses? People who stop living and enjoying life have replaced all of that with excuses. Excuses of worry or worthiness, judgement of others, laziness, or coming up with something to do. You used to just go out and do, then slowly you stopped. Think back, you didn't even have the resources, or reliable friends, but you went out and had experiences anyway. You ended up around different people, new places. Your comfort zone didn't really make much of a difference. Why can't you revisit that part of you again? Be spontaneous. You are letting life pass you by and you don't have to. Why are you holding back? Why are you choosing to be home and miserable? Your health would be less of a concern if you were active in life and shifted your focus. Unlock your cage and remind yourself what freedom feels like.

You must keep learning to experience growth and to evolve. It's how you stay curious and explore new ideas and parts of yourself. It doesn't even matter what you decide to study or learn as it all enhances your experience and keeps your mind growing and your opportunities expanding. The format can also vary as different people learn or pay attention better in different settings and formats. You could watch lectures, interviews, or documentaries. You can take courses online or in person. You could read books, attend summits, weekend retreats, or emersion events, yoga, meditation, or sound healing. You can receive healing sessions, past life readings, tarot, or channeled messages.

There are so many resources and opportunities it doesn't matter which you gravitate toward. They are all opportunities for expansion to learn more about the Universe and yourself, to connect to yourself, others, or the unknown. You just need to know there are opportunities out there and you can always grow, change, and become the person you were always meant to be. The obstacles start to disappear once you start to give yourself the knowledge and opportunities needed for transformation and change.

You can't stay the same and then wonder why you are bored or stagnant in life, or why you feel like you are in a routine. The only way to get out of that is to explore, develop, and try new things. Your access to information is very accessible these days with tv and internet. You have so many more resources that other generations never had. See what's out there. See what you can become. You don't even need to set goals to learn and obtain understanding of something new. Learning has no limits. You expand as you go and learning one thing will often lead to you exploring or questioning other things and learning about them. It eventually creates a path, connects the dots, leads you to where you need to be going. Information will find its way to you once you are open to receiving it. The only thing you need to do is be open.

That does not mean automatically believe or trust everything you learn. But that's the great thing about learning. You choose. You get to choose what you keep and what you discard. What makes sense and what does not pertain to how you want to interpret or live your life. It's about opening doors, but you still get to choose if you walk through them and how far into the space you want to explore.

You cannot have growth without knowledge, and you cannot gain knowledge if you are closed. When you stop allowing new information in is when you ultimately stop growing. There are many who are this way and accept what they learned already as facts and deny any information that says otherwise. They have chosen to lock the door of personal growth and stay where they are. Life is about choices. Growth is a choice. You can learn more and enhance your experience or stay where you are. But it's always a choice, and that choice is always yours.

Shifting is important and it's going to keep coming up more as you evolve as a test to see where you are and to make sure you are aware and incorporating what you learn. It's one thing to learn about concepts and how things work. It's another to put them into action and incorporate these changes into your life. View it as an exciting challenge and opportunity. Don't fall back into stress and despair. That is your old default and that's what we are trying to change. Take a minute if you need to for whatever emotions or reactions surface. But limit how much time you give them and then move on. Your feelings let you know where you still are in the process. Have they changed any or are they still as negative as they were previously?

This is an opportunity to adjust and incorporate what you've been learning, for you to control the trajectory and then surrender to a higher power to push you through. But you need to set the course first and be aware of what your views and reactions are. Don't let life stress you out. Find why it feels that way and address that. This is the only way you will start to have better outcomes.

This is how personal development works. This is how you know where you are in the present so you can adjust for the future. If you are still in a paradigm of lack and worry, then you can't be surprised when those are your results with your savings account and business. Until you fix where you are coming from and break those chains you aren't going to stray far from the same results you have always had. It takes time and effort to break a habit physically and sometimes more so mentally. But the work needs to be done. It will improve your life, making you strong and providing an example to teach others how to do the same. Speak your truth, don't shut down when asked questions.

What are you aware of and how are you using it? Implement your learning. That is the only way it is useful and not just words you read.

IT'S NOT A CHORE. IT'S EVOLUTION

What are you doing with it? How are you harvesting what you are growing. Are you sharing, letting it rot back into the ground, or making the most of what you are given? You get to choose how you incorporate things and the results you see. Set goals and routines. Choose one new piece of info and use it in your daily life. Hiding it in a notebook for reference doesn't get the work done. Don't overload. Choose one thing at a time and address it. What do you want to work on first? Stay focused. See what you are capable of. Get excited about possibilities and go after them. Transform your life and see where it takes you. You could surprise yourself with how much easier it will become once you start doing the work instead of just listening to the assignment.

Notice what comes up. What's distracting you? What self-talk is happening? Find out the source and clear a path. You must make room for the new that is to come. Replace what needs to go with what will better serve you. You've had so much change already. Write down what has shifted. Be grateful for what is developing. You might be surprised at how far you've come when you actually put your awareness on where you are now and where you started. See the changes as momentum that you are worthy and keep going.

Is it a broken record or the repetition needed to learn? The record gets broken only after you play it enough that you know the lyrics and recognize the scratches as part of the song. How often do you hear the same outlook before seeing through those eyes? Make things your own. Realize the importance of what you are doing. Follow the steps. Don't just listen to the words. You cannot build a new life without breaking the soil and getting your hands dirty. You need to lay it out brick by brick. How determined are you to get it done? How badly do you want a new life?

You need to want it enough to see it for yourself, to want to know what it feels like, to visualize it as a possibility, to have the courage to take the steps when they show up along your path. You can't want something new and refuse to do something new to achieve it. You don't need a clear goal. You just need a general one with enough details. As you get closer and realize your capabilities the picture will become clearer and come into focus. The excitement for what you are building will grow along with the vision. How could you clearly see something that might not even exist yet, whose conception is still in the process of being realized? Move toward it. Be curious. Poke at it till it perforates and sheds light upon what you are doing, and the dream becomes fully realized. Your faith in yourself plays a large role in what you will find on the other side of progress. What are you really capable of? Who are you?

Come out of your comfort zone, the routines, the habits. See what works and what doesn't. Make a plan for change and stick to it. If you aren't happy with things, change them. That's all it takes to get back on course and set things right. You need to have awareness and determination to follow through. It's the follow through that's important otherwise you are just standing still. Actions equal progress. Inactions equal a rut. Which are you allocating your time to? Which are you prioritizing and basing your life around?

You can hear the same advice and same words repeatedly but until you acknowledge, accept, and make changes they won't do you any good. Can you see your life different than it is? If you can't, why is that? How hard are you willing to push through that to make it to the other side and change that belief? Does it really matter where it came from? No. It's just a starting point. Knowing it's there will allow you to start from there and proceed into something you want instead.

What do you really want? It's not going to just magically appear. You need to do work on some level. It could be fixing belief systems, your views, or simple habits in your life. It's not always hard steps but you do need to put in the time and find something that works to help you flip your habits into something healthier. What do you want to see in your life? How badly do you want to see it? How long will you push off the life you really want? What are you waiting for?

———

Be open to new lessons and learning. See how you feel and react to new information and different ways of living. Why do you feel how you feel? Is it a choice or brought about by something or someone else? Work on listening without worrying about what to say next or how to relate. Just be and really listen. Implement some of your new teachings. See how it feels around a trusted friend when judgment is not there. Where is your acceptance level? Are you choosing your options because it makes life easier or because it's really what you want? How are you really letting yourself down? Notice in your life when you changed your path due to peer pressure rather than what was your path or what felt right to you. You are an adult now and can think about your choices with a clear mind. What do you see? What has changed? What needs to change?

Reflect on things the way they are, and how they were. Look for patterns, growth, and repeated mistakes. Learn to understand yourself so you know what is or isn't working. This is a big step in personal development. See the truth, acknowledge it, and then do something about it in a constructive manner.

What do you really want to see in your life and how focused are you on the work needed to get there. The work needs to be done if change is ever going to happen. Otherwise, it's just busy work. The student needs to become professional at some point and put the learning to use. What do you want to become? Let others see what you know you are capable of. Own it. You're working hard for it.

You need to be brave no matter the circumstances. Fear is just an illusion made up in your mind. You talk yourself out of things that you could easily do if you tried, learned, and put forth effort. Courage comes from within. It's the ability to see past all the excuses and move forward with the awareness and knowledge that failure is just an opportunity to learn and fear is just an excuse. You can do anything and the only thing standing in your way is yourself and your beliefs. Be brave and see what comes of it. You can't move forward without stepping out of your comfort zone. How badly do you want a new future. Are you willing to step through your own self-doubt and negative self-talk to get it? Will you be your own hero and walk through challenges with confidence and conviction? How strong are you mentally? Can you push through your own excuses and see them as just that, excuses?

Be the support system you need. If you can't rely on yourself then all trust is broken. You can be your own guiding light, your own hero. You just need to believe in yourself and be willing to do the work to get what you want. Will you persevere or sit and stare? It's your life. It's your choice. Be brave. You have pushed through so much already that you don't even give yourself credit for it. Look how far you've come. Look how strong you are now mentally. Use your voice. There's no more hiding. You must be seen. You must be heard. You are important. Gather up your courage and move forward in life. You've got this.

Be prepared for change, open to new opportunities, for development. The steps might not make sense now, but they are parts of the puzzle we are building. One idea leads to another until breakthroughs happen and goals are reached. You just need to take those steps and keep moving even if you are unsure of the direction, they are leading. There needs to be trust in the higher purpose of where this is all going. Questioning it will only delay progress. It might not make sense now but like most things, when you look back you see where it was an important step on the journey.

Be patient. You can't be in a rush to get somewhere when you aren't clear where the destination is. Trust when you lift your foot the ground will be firm when you place it back down. The next steps will arrive after the learning or experiences have happened that are needed for the next leg of the journey. Keep doing as you are doing, learning, and connecting the dots. You are in the re-educating yourself stage as the ability to understand, release, or connect outside of yourself are of value for what you will be doing.

Learn acceptance, trust, and non-judgement. See where it's frustrating you and why that is holding you back. Find its source and release it or forget about its source and release it from here and move forward. But you must address it, so it won't keep holding you to outdated ideas, or limited thinking. View it from outside of yourself. Don't let everything pull at you or frustrate you. There is strength in letting go. You've come this far. Keep the path clear and keep going. The path will open, and you'll see the destination soon enough.

You have to be passionate about something to push through the distractions or other things that are vying for your time. If you aren't driven, it will not happen. Passion and drive almost go together in that way. One creates the other. If you have passion, you are driven towards it. If you are driven towards something, you are often passionate about it. Find out what you are passionate about and see how often you are pulled toward it and accomplish tasks related to it, like music, learning, or drawing. There are many things that pull at you, and you find joy in or get excited about. This is how you start to learn what you should be doing or what your journey is about. Your life's purpose can't be connected to something you aren't driven or passionate about. You need that spark to push you into things. Others will see that spark when you talk about it, or experience activities related to it. If that spark is not there maybe, you shouldn't be there either.

Find what calls you and answer it. Find what is taking up your time that doesn't and prioritize accordingly. Don't spend your days strapped to something you don't enjoy when you could be doing something you are passionate about. Find a way to make it work for what you need. If it's work, you don't enjoy, find a way to turn your passion into your income. It might take some effort, but wouldn't it be nice to wake up excited about what you are doing, instead of watching the clock? Find what needs adjusting and adjust it. This is your life. You should be enjoying it.

———

Seek and ye shall find. You must explore or research to educate yourself about the truth, to find out who you really are, to find the answers to the hard questions. There is effort that needs to happen for growth to be obtained. It's up to you to decide how much, how often, and the subject. Personal growth and development start with you. You can't have more or different until you add that into the mix. How much do you really understand? Are you looking for an overview or enough to explain it to someone else? What pulls on your interests? How can it be incorporated into your life? Where is it leading you? Sometimes they are just steps to help you understand something much bigger down the road. But you need to do the work now, to have the interest, take the initiative, and grow upon things.

IT'S NOT A CHORE. IT'S EVOLUTION

Knowledge is not wasted. Understanding is not wasted. But do understand when you are trying to dive too deep into something that is not meant for you and shift your focus accordingly. It's not supposed to cause you mental irritation trying to comprehend something. Your ability to understand or not understand doesn't cause something not to exist. It just makes it not a focus for your attention. See what is out there that can help you build the life you want. What is calling to you that could enhance what you already know or feel? There is mastery in understanding. What have you been missing? What part of you is wanting to be brought to the surface? What could you be explaining to others to ease tensions in their lives? Find your truth and keep going. The world is yours to explore. Go out and see what you find.

You familiarize yourself with the area, the location, the scenery, the feeling, and the landscape; Internal and external. You learn it, inside and out, where it becomes second nature, familiar, a part of you. You will then become the compass, the guide for your journey. You cannot become lost within that which is a part of you, is inside of you, is you.

The path taken is not of consequence. It's that you are on a path, that you are seeking, experiencing, learning, gaining traction. The destination is the same. It's a matter of how or when the circumstances of the journey will change for everyone. But we are all on a journey. We're treading the landscape, getting our feet wet. We're making strides to get somewhere. The path may not be clear, but that is part of the thrill. Seeing what's ahead, the surprises, things gained, people met, experiences shared.

Flip the mind from seeing everything as an obstacle in your way, instead view it as a ladder to get further ahead. How can this be used to benefit the journey? It's a found object lying in wait to be repurposed instead of discarded. Everything found is a gain, always of use, never to be discarded or left behind. You want to keep that path clear for those who will follow, or whoever comes across the clearing you made.

You may rest as needed, or even take a detour. But you will never get anywhere if you decide to head back. That is no longer a direction you can go. You have learned what you needed from that location. It is now grown over and is more difficult to walk back through so you must move forward. Realize how strong you are to be doing this. See how far you have come. You may surprise yourself if you take notice of where you have been, what you have learned, and how you have grown. Your blossoms, your seeds, your roots are grounded, planted firmly to help you stay strong. Be a beacon of joy, of hope, of strength for those still working their way down their own path.

It's your own version of, I was here. We are connected, you can do this too. It's not impossible. You have unlimited strength to pull from, unlimited resources to guide you, and unlimited help ready for when you reach out for it. There is always a hand to pull you up when you forget how capable you are of standing on your own two feet. Just stand up. Look up. See where you are and shine. Become that beacon, a compass for all.

POETRY

Eruption of Change

Rumbling and shaking,

Like a volcano about to spill over.

Scorching the surface.

Burning the old to make room for the new.

New and improved.

Improving upon a firm foundation, already built.

Just building upon, adding to, making more.

Not necessarily of the same.

Same old thoughts, beliefs, ideas,

but transforming those that must go.

Aerating the ground for new growth,

For new ideas, new paths, rivers, streams.

Going with the flow.

Getting caught up in the current.

Current to currency,

Abundance that is to come,

Switching it up,

Up to you how it starts to look once the transformation happens.

But happen, it must.

It is time.

This has all risen from below and was ready to come to the surface.

To be released.

Release your expectations, your restraints, your boundaries.

Let it go to let this become what it can without directing the path.

Thinking you know better than the Universal flow of thoughts, ideas, lessons.

Clear a path.

Make room,.

Never stay stuck in what is,

When you could live in the possibilities of what could be instead.

Open the gap wider,

Allow for more to seep out and spill over.

Running down the surface.

Making its way down.

Picking up speed.

Forging ahead

Creating new roads to travel, places to be, people to meet.

Let it all come to the surface,

IT'S NOT A CHORE. IT'S EVOLUTION

Explode into a frenzy of activity and watch the transformation happen.

See what new will grow once you clear the debris and see the beauty in the change.

Don't miss out!

Visit the website below and you can sign up to receive emails whenever Michelle Syner publishes a new book. There's no charge and no obligation.

https://books2read.com/r/B-A-YFIX-OVWQC

BOOKS 2 READ

Connecting independent readers to independent writers.

About the Author

Michelle Syner is a channel for automatic writing who attends classes, lectures, summits, and workshops for Personal and Spiritual Development. She is a Reconnective Healing Foundational & Reconnection-Certified Practitioner and founder Lightwork Restorations. For additional information or to find out more about her offerings visit www.LightworkRestorations.com

Read more at https://lightworkrestorations.com/.

www.ingramcontent.com/pod-product-compliance
Lightning Source LLC
Chambersburg PA
CBHW060538160726
47991CB00001B/373